AF824405

Praise for the Book

"*'The Enlightened Lawyer' echoes the Psalms, revealing surfing as a path to spiritual purification. From Malibu's waves to Talmudic tradition, the ocean offers redemption where materialism fails. Dale's journey reflects society's moral drift, yet surfing restores the soul. This book is a call to holistic living—part memoir, part manual for redemption. A powerful testament to life beyond greed, Attorney David Olan's work deserves a place on every lawyer's shelf.*"

—Shaloha, Rabbi Nachum Shifren,
Author of *Surfing Rabbi & Surfers Who Don't Surf*

"*'The Enlightened Lawyer' by Dave Olan is a gripping blend of legal drama, spiritual awakening, and oceanic healing. It follows attorney Dale Owen's fall from legal success into moral collapse, triggered by a destructive romance and personal vices. His redemption begins with the guidance of a mystical Buddha figure who imparts three transformative techniques. Through nature's healing—especially the sea—and spiritual insight, Dale finds renewal. Olan's novel is both inspiring and instructive, offering a powerful message of balance, resilience, and inner peace in a demanding world.*"

—James Carr,
International Trial Lawyer

"'The Enlightened Lawyer' is an inspiring story of redemption, following Dale Owen—a successful but egocentric attorney whose life unravels through toxic choices and a destructive romance. Consumed by status, power, and shallow relationships, Dale's downfall is swift and painful. At rock bottom, he encounters a mystical Buddha and the ocean's healing power, sparking a deep spiritual transformation. With honesty, insight, and heart, 'The Enlightened Lawyer' invites readers to reflect on their own lives—and discover that within each of us lies the power to change, to heal, and to live more meaningfully."

—Lauryn Boston, Attorney/Mediator, Long-Time Maui Resident, and Buddhist, Co-creator of John from Cincinnati and Chance, Writer on HBO's Deadwood and FX's Sons of Anarchy

"In this remarkable fusion of surfing wisdom and legal insight, Dave Olan masterfully draws from his pioneering work as founder of the Association of Surfing Lawyers to deliver profound life lessons. The Enlightened Lawyer transcends traditional self-help boundaries, offering three transformative techniques that bridge the gap between professional success and spiritual fulfillment. As someone who witnessed the early days of ASL and its evolution into a global movement, I can attest to Olan's unique ability to translate the meditative power of riding waves into practical wisdom for navigating life's challenges. This compelling narrative isn't just for legal professionals or surf enthusiasts—it's an inspirational roadmap for anyone seeking deeper meaning and authentic fulfillment in their journey."

—Shaun Tomson, World Champion Surfer,
Inspirational Speaker, Author of *Surfer's Code*,
Owner of Instinct Surf Company

Buddha Fields for Attorneys

The Enlightened Lawyer

Three Priceless Techniques to Transform Your Life

David Olan & Daniel O'Hara

Global Book Publishing

The Enlightened Lawyer
David Olan & Daniel O'Hara
©2025 David Olan & Daniel O'Hara
All rights reserved.

All rights reserved. No part of this publication may be reproduced, distributed, or transmitted in any form or by any means, including photocopying, recording, or other electronic or mechanical methods, without the prior written permission of the author or publisher (except by a reviewer, who may quote brief passages and/or show brief video clips in a review).

ISBN: 978-1-964644-44-8
Book Design & Publishing done by:
Global Book Publishing
www.globalbookpublishing.com

Disclaimer: No part of this publication may be reproduced, stored in a retrieval system, or transmitted in any form or by any means, mechanical, electronic, photocopying, recording, or otherwise, without the prior written permission of the publisher and the author. The Publisher and the Authors make no representations or warranties with respect to the accuracy and completeness of this work and especially disclaim all warranties, including without limitation warranties of fitness for a particular purpose. No warranty may be created or extended by sales or promotional materials. The advice and strategies contained herein may not be suitable for every situation. This work is sold with the understanding that the Publisher is not engaged in rendering legal, accounting, or other professional services. If professional assistance is required, the services of a competent professional person should be sought. Neither the Publisher nor the Author shall be liable for the damages arising herefrom.

From David Olan:

This book is dedicated to all lawyers, surfers, and soul-searchers. My life has been filled with an abundance of love from family and friends. I wouldn't know where to begin thanking people as my heart is filled with gratitude for the amazingly supportive relationships I have forged since early childhood. I am grateful to the spiritual gurus I have encountered in my life and the guidance provided by them in person or in writing.

In particular, I want to thank Daniel O'Hara for his inspiration in creating the "Buddha Fields," featuring the Three Priceless Techniques and inspiring/goading me to write "The Enlightened Lawyer" about eight years ago and Ben Marcus for his wit, insight, and editing skills.

Also, I must mention my son Curren (whose namesake is indeed Tom Curren, my friend and cool Californian musician and three-times World Champion surfer). My son is the balancing force in my life. He is funny, grounded, shreds on guitar, and his creative spirit got him into the Parsons School of Design in Paris. He starts school there as this book is being published.

I appreciate all of the great people who reviewed this transcript and submitted testimonials. It has been a labor of love indeed.

From Daniel O'Hara:

This book is dedicated to David Olan, who invested eight years in its creation, weaving his vast experiences into the vision of an Enlightened Lawyer.

It is also dedicated to my extraordinary son, Austin-John Patrick O'Hara, who, from a young age, displayed the qualities of a successful lawyer. His profound soul positions him as a future torchbearer for Enlightened Lawyers, destined to illuminate the world of law and build upon the legacy David pioneered.

Table of Contents

Opening Statement

Counselors and members of the jury, approach this book with great skepticism. Your skepticism is healthy in your business practice, especially when looking for incongruences in one's testimony.

In reading this book, however, let your experience be your guide. The scales of justice balance the rational and the experiential. People know the *Buddha Fields* series as *experience* books, as the reader lives vicariously through the trials and tribulations of the relatable main character and may gain thirty years of wisdom in only a few hours.

Again, while not legal advice, it is easily worth thousands of dollars per hour invested in reading it. With each reading, you will gain more insights and experiences.

The Enlightened Lawyer is relatable and funny, and Gerry Spence is worthy of the information provided, yet the Buddha's sagaciousness will also help you improve every area of your life.

Vajrayana Buddhism (aka Tantric or *The Method*) will introduce you to the concept of *skillful means.* This book, when applied, will significantly accelerate your spiritual growth. Meditative and spiritual practices like the *Buddha Fields Blessing Meditation, ESSENTIAL Buddhist Practices Seminar, and the BUDDHAFICATION Master Class* are *available at www.DanielPOHara.com and will take you to the next level,* helping you to put into practice what you've learned.

Please get on our email list for the upcoming Enlightened Lawyer Seminars at www.EnlightenedLawyer.com

"*There are only two mistakes one can make along the road to truth; not starting and not going all the way.*"

—Buddha

Foreword

You've seen *Point Break*—the 1991 classic directed by Kathryn Bigelow, which stars Keanu Reeves as Johnny Utah, Lori Petty as Tyler, Gary Busey as the burnt-out FBI agent Pappas, and Patrick Swayze as Bodhi, the charismatic leader of a gang of bank robbers who take scores wearing the masks of dead presidents. Among them, surf legend John "Turtle" Philbin plays Nathanial in a Jimmy Carter mask. In one memorable scene after a sand football game, undercover lawman Johnny aggressively tackles Bodhi and stirs unrest among the group, who rush to confront him at the water's edge. When they realize Johnny was an all-conference college football hero, the dynamic quickly changes.

> "*I know, Dave! I've surfed with Dave, and he was cool out in the lineup! And Dave won me a lot of money in a lawsuit when I lost everything in the Woolsey fire in Malibu! I like Dave, he's a lawyer who surfs!*"

—John Philbin,
aka Turtle from North Shore,
aka Nathanial from Point Break

ROACH

Jesus Christ! Johnny fuckin' Utah!

Sorry, man. Didn't mean to get in ya' face!

BODHI

I knew I knew you. It was the Rose Bowl.

Three years ago, you beat SC.

TANK GIRL

You? You did this?

BODHI

Yep, him!

ROACH

That was one hell of a game.

GROMMET

No shit.

BODHI

Yeah, but you got nuked in the last quarter.

JOHNNY UTAH

Yeah, I got my knee folded back about 90 degrees the wrong way!

BODHI

Whoa! That's why you never went pro?

JOHNNY UTAH

Two years of surgery, missed my window.

Went to law school instead.

BODHI

Law school! You're a lawyer? Wow!

Well, life's not over yet, man. You're surfing.

NATHANIAL

Lawyers don't surf!

BODHI

This one does.[1]

In the minds of many, lawyers don fancy suits, drive luxury cars, and lead structured lives filled with deadlines and stress, earning billable hours and debating cases in stuffy courtrooms. Meanwhile, carefree and adventurous surfers eschew the material world, and spend most of their time catching waves instead of reading legal briefs.

But the truth is, many lawyers also surf; after all, surfing is an outlet for the physical and mental stress lawyers endure, and offers risk management, opportunity, and resilience, qualities that are indispensable in both law and life.

Lawyers don't surf?

Lawyers *should* surf.

Dave Olan, known for his involvement in Malibu's surf culture and legal achievements, has balanced both worlds remarkably. With roots in a legal family, he pursued his own career, earning accolades like Best Lawyers' and Super Lawyers' recognition and contributing significantly to the legal community. Olan founded the US Association of Surfing Lawyers, combining his love for law and surfing.

---

[1] "Point Break," James Cameron & Kathryn Bigelow; from the screenplay by W. Peter Iliff, 1991. This scene extract is excerpted from the movie script; all rights to the original composition, recordings, and lines are reserved by the writers, directors, and distributors.

Enlightened Lawyer: Three Priceless Techniques to Transform Your Life explores the intense stresses of legal practice while celebrating the rejuvenating power of surfing. Our narrator, Dale Owen, recounts Olan's intricate legal and emotional journey, a path that leads him into a tumultuous romance that threatens his career and personal stability.

Dale Owen might have found himself one of the "suckers born every minute," but Enlightened Lawyer is a finely tuned tale of rebirth and personal growth, in which Dale finds his spiritual footing and rides the wave of his life.

His journey includes an adrenaline-fueled reimagining of Shakespeare's The Tempest, as the 1611 version of Only a Surfer Knows the Feeling.

Full fathom five thy father lies;
Of his bones are coral made;
Those are pearls that were his eyes:
Nothing of him that doth fade,
But doth suffer a sea-change
Into something rich and strange.
Sea-nymphs hourly ring his knell:
Ding-dong.
Hark! Now I hear them,— ding-dong, bell.[2]

"*Ultimately, Enlightened Lawyer illuminates one man's struggle with the temptations of modern life, and a quest for redemption guided by teachings that reshape his perspective on life and law. Dale's journey reaffirms surfing as profoundly restorative, and a practice that many attorneys, like Owen, could benefit from embracing.*"

—James Webster, Aussie Surfing/ Tennis-Playing Brilliant Trial Lawyer

[2] William Shakespeare, The Tempest, Act 1, Scene 2. "Full fathom five thy father lies" is taken from Ariel's song (second paragraph) in this scene. As the work of William Shakespeare, this text is in the public domain.

CHAPTER 1

The Crisis

With that same shock and awe one felt watching hijacked planes hit the World Trade Center, then Uncle Sam payback-bombing Baghdad, my life exploded and imploded and went up in smoke today. Like the Twin Towers—which had seemed so sturdy and untouchable—everything I cared about, everything I'd been working for all along, gone; collapsed into smoke and ash. My professional life, the respect of my colleagues, my standing in the community, the money I earned, the love for which I'd risked everything—my entire life as I'd known it up to that point—gone like a puff of smoke.

Shocked and awful, the reality and consequences too much to bear, I gag a little, cover my mouth quickly to keep that bit of vomit from leaving my mouth, and swallow it back down. My head throbs, my vision blurs, and the world I once saw at home in is now a surreal, untouchable, parallel universe.

I shake my head, trying to rid myself of the cobwebs. It doesn't work. My name is still Dale Owen Esq., but my identity and world have changed into Dale Owen NotForHire. My training and experience as an attorney should prepare me for this. It should prepare me for anything. I'd seen other people destroy their lives and helped them through it. But now, I am the victim.

How the hell did I get here? This isn't supposed to happen to people like me.

Like a cross-examining attorney, I put myself through a round of interrogation. What do I know? Let's look at the evidence, counselor. I am certainly Dale Owen. Perhaps you've heard of me. Oh, no, I'm not famous, but amongst people worth knowing… Wait, that doesn't sound right at all. I'm sure I can find a more viable beginning.

I was born and raised to be a lawyer. It's all I've ever known. My meteoric rise at a family firm may not sound very impressive to you, but I did some exceptional work those first seven and a half years out of law school. I had been both practical and lucky, and Owen & Owen made me an equity partner in that embarrassingly short amount of time. Owen & Owen, Owen & Owen, it's like a hypnotist's trigger to me now, and God knows where the mere thought of those sounds will take me at any given moment. In my mind, those syllables no longer simply evoke the silk-stocking LA law firm that had been our family business for as long as I could remember. They add up to a specter now, and I don't know how to shake it.

The beginning of my end was supposed to be just another client interview, but nothing prepared me for what was to come. I can be intuitive, but not this time. No cold sweats, no sinking feeling in the gut, no strangely unaccounted-for change in room temperature, none of the signals that I had previously experienced warning me of DANGER.

Her name was Bianca, Bianca de la Rosa. She had a company named Biotrimus. They made some kind of energy/diet pill, which was produced and marketed as a dietary supplement—that is, not a drug—so no FDA approval was required. Leaving out the FDA certainly simplified matters. I should have smelled something fishy when the notes for the meeting stated that a former client of mine, whom she'd met briefly at the gym, had referred her. She couldn't remember his name but remembered mine—the first of many, many red flags that I waved off.

I should have smelled a rat, but at the time of our first client consultation, all I could smell was her unusually fragrant perfume.

A snapshot of the matter, as I understood it, was that a distributor was claiming Biotrimus was in breach of an agreement for having failed to fulfill an order. Bianca came in with her business partner, John Sonders, and I was flabbergasted, an absolute deer in the headlights. Bianca was so gorgeous, I had to perform a mental search to see if I'd ever seen such a stunningly beautiful woman in my life. I was momentarily tongue-tied, couldn't really pay attention, trying to remember anyone prettier. I regained my composure enough to remind myself that I was a lawyer and should, at the very least, turn on my attorney's autopilot.

Apparently, this unknown gym-goer had highly recommended me, and she *looked me up,* stating she was so impressed by my reputation and accomplishments. The meeting went just fine after that. Bianca did most of the talking anyway, and it wasn't long before I realized she was not just extraordinarily pretty but extraordinary in every sense: bright, ambitious, and radiantly charming. I mean, wow, she knew how to work it! Work *me.* I felt elated but also kind of nervous when I met someone I thought I could fall in love with. Those butterflies weren't just flying around down there. They were playing a lovely ballad on a harp.

I grew up in Brentwood, California, with a silver spoon in my mouth. Bianca did not. If what she said was true, her mother was an American of Guatemalan descent, and she proudly boasted of her father's 100% Peruvian pedigree. She told me she'd grown up primarily in Arizona and graduated from the U of A with a Bachelor of Science in biology. She also said she got her MBA at Pepperdine, which made me wonder how I could have possibly never seen this vision of a person if she had been floating around Malibu for at least a few years. When we met, she claimed she was thirty-seven and looked about twenty-eight or maybe even twenty-four. I'd noticed how perfect her body was when she came in, then corrected myself because, no, it was better than perfect. It was music. Sweet, sweet music with a Latin beat!

Her olive skin and fine jawline were the mantles for her bizarre brown eyes that popped like topaz. I believe there was more than one moment in which I managed, I hope discreetly, to adjust both my posture and my thoughts enough to try to at least look like I was listening to her, none of which lasted long. I was so overwhelmed that, to this day, what I recall most vividly about the meeting was repeatedly trying to regain my cool and failing, trailing off into dreamland.

Once again, I moved around to compose myself, this time resolving finally to get down to business. I came to my senses enough to roll through what we might do for her—I have no idea what I actually said—tell her what a pleasure it was to meet her and her partner as mildly as possible and hand her back to my secretary to sign her up and collect a $10,000 retainer as if I had something important to do. Alone in my office after she left, even though she was still in the building finishing up, I imagined a winged chariot descending to pick her up in front of the building and whisk her away back to heaven. Valhalla. Wherever sweet angels return to.

Their retainer cleared, and I initiated an aggressive defense on behalf of Bianca and John. We demurred to the complaint, unloaded a nasty boatload of discovery, and then noticed everyone's deposition. Two weeks after that, I called the opposing attorney to subtly threaten and insult him—just par for the course—and take his temperature on the case. After some bluster and sparring back-and-forth, again, at par, the case settled very much in our favor three or four weeks later.

Once the case was over, Bianca was not only relieved and elated but also grateful. Mm-hmm. She and John were anxious about public exposure, not to mention the expense of litigation. John was grateful, too, and quite complimentary, but I wasn't very interested in his gratitude.

Their account had a $5,700 unpaid balance, and I waived it. Although our billing procedures were excessive anyway, I'd never done anything like that before, and my father came in to reprimand me. Sure, there are times when there is a small balance left on either a big case we'd already billed plenty on or some hopelessly lost cause that was never going to be paid anyway, and the firm could write off viable losses like that. I told him, "I'm sorry, Dad. I have no excuse for this except that I think I'm in love with her." For once, he made a joke about money. Bianca caused quite a stir around the office, too, mostly with the men. He pointed his finger at me, said, "Don't do it again!" and walked out, leaving me to figure out whether he was talking about falling in love with a client or waiving collectible fees. This was the beginning of things going wrong for good between my father and me, but I remember that, at least that day, he treated me like a man and let it be.

Clearly, her talent was immense, but it didn't take much of it for me to accept Bianca's invitation to a "celebration" lunch. I suggested a terrific, quaint little café near the office called "La Canción." It had great food and a warm atmosphere. I was friendly with the chef, and it was just far enough off the beaten path. It seemed to be a suitable response to her not-so-business-like invitation to a client lunch. Lunch, for me, usually meant obnoxiously overpriced joints one goes to see and be seen—just as part of doing business. I remember something fishy in Denmark, since it seemed like too ridiculous a fantasy that a woman like that would have anything more than a business interest in a guy like me. But I also thought I'd better take my shot. Just the chance to be alone with her in this charming joint would be its own dream come true.

Then, a few days later, when I heard John was joining us, the fantasy turned cold, embarrassing, and moribund. It was downright depressing. Yet, Bianca was the only one sitting there the day I was shown to our table. It was all I could do to keep the dribble in my mouth. The short skirt, part of a slammin' black suit, had a pleat in the middle that allowed me to see up to the top of her thigh along the slit with her right leg crossed over the other. Her exquisite calves glistened, shaped as if Michelangelo had molded them.

As I approached the table, she rose to greet me, looking at me straight with those big brown eyes, saying musically, "Hi, Dale," and planting a ripe kiss on my left cheek—hugging me just enough to get very aroused. Then, she stared at me briefly, that wily smile coupled with a hypnotic gaze from those topaz eyes until she realized she'd smeared me with a bit of lipstick, mocked a frown, and wiped the lipstick off with her thumb, nice and rough.

Not long after we'd settled in, Bianca explained that she and John were just business partners. She said it again—*just* business partners and friends—in a way that seemed to imply something I wasn't quite sure of. Is he gay? Is he impotent? Is he stupid? I didn't completely get it, but then she took my hand and looked me in the eye—no lipstick problem this time and gave me a smile that shone. I recall the chills I felt down my spine. Something was going to happen between us.

We were—as the kids say here in the twenty-first century: vibing.

Bianca was so completely engaging with me, so winning, that I would have done anything for her from that moment until it all came crashing down. Oh, how my energy level soared! I had never been much of a drug user beyond weed and drink, but I was already sure, sitting with her in that café, I would have walked down the darkest alley to get this drug, and ultimately did. I had simply experienced nothing like that before. The playful gaze, her touching me more often than she should have, the feigned big laughs at my jokes, the shower of compliments about what a *take-charge guy* I was, and *brilliant,* no less! She made me, and I was melting like butter on a hot summer day.

Of course, it was strictly against firm policy for attorneys to date clients and certainly frowned upon by the State Bar, which is a far more complicated remark than you might imagine. That was—at the time. Subsequently, the bar changed its *Canons of Ethics,* making it a cause for discipline. In the weeks to come, my father would have something more to say about it than his cleverness. But I told myself that her legal matter had been settled, a few technical details notwithstanding, and we began seeing each other seriously almost immediately after that lunch. This was a handy excuse and not untrue, but even if we were still deep into her matter or some other matter involving her, after those signals, I'm sure I would have come up with some way to rationalize putting myself into this clearly compromised position. I mean, look at her!

CHAPTER 2

Bianca Blitz

Early on and for a good while, Bianca's behavior led me to believe that she was this miraculously patient, kind, attentive person who was somehow fascinated by my every move and utterance. As you laugh, think of my shame at having to write out that sentence. The miracle within my tragic delusions about her was that she could also be so passionate about life. In light of all that's happened, sure. But, really, even though she was a conman, she was still biting into life for all it was worth, or so it seemed.

Look, what the hell did I know then? I continued to be that kid in the candy shop—what a joy to wake up every morning.

Outside the house, it filled me with pride to show her off to friends, family, and strangers—everyone. Parading into the hippest places in town with the hottest girl in the city or any place at all had me walking on air. Suddenly, people realized how charming and interesting *I* was! Suddenly, *I* had moves! *I* put the *me* in the *game*. Not really, of course. It was more that people wanted to be near her, and no one was getting nearer to her than I was (that I knew of), so her ability to evoke that almost universal desire to feel her heat, to look into those eyes, rubbed off on me a bit.

I was so proud of myself that my ego took in a bit more air every day. I stood taller. Just about everyone who saw her wanted a piece of her, so, male or female, heads turned wherever we went, and those heads came to understand that she was coming home with me just about every night.

Much too late, I realized that the first meeting was just a trap. I was her prey, and I didn't even know it. Instead of seeing it, I fell head over heels in love with her. It's humiliating how soon I opened up to her. Before I'd met her, I was used to guarding my thoughts and feelings because I'm a fucking lawyer. My father was a lawyer, and his father was a lawyer. Gramps was supposedly a paragon of virtue and ethics and all that crap.

With this girl on my arm and my place in the firm, it felt like a superhero thing, and I wasn't just a lawyer. I was the Lawyer Clark Kent, ripping off my suit. I was now a Super Lawyer!

Perhaps the main thing that built me up so high was how amazing it felt to have someone so extraordinary listen and really want to be with me. Bianca said she thought she had found the perfect guy. Me? Yes! As a result, I became much nicer, exceedingly to her, of course, but very much so as I went through my day. For a while, at least, I may not have been the nicest guy before I met Bianca. While the good part lasted, I felt happy inside, as good as I had felt in my entire life. I didn't take my work so seriously anymore, which I was about to begin to pay for. But there was something else in my world, and it was no longer just about poor me. I was really in love with someone. Staff and associates weren't scurrying off when I came along like they used to. I barked orders less than I used to. I just started talking to people about what we were working on.

So, yes, I began to tell Bianca everything about my life. My thoughts, fears, dreams, industry secrets, and secrets within the firm. Oy. I told her all the good stories and so many vignettes from my life, like we start to tell any new lover, and she remembered them and asked sweetly or teased me about them later. It felt like she really wanted to know me, and I believed she did.

Bianca was a workout freak. She usually went to the gym twice or thrice a day for one to two hours, five days a week, sometimes more. As you may know, she was not just the owner of Biotrimus, but also its spokesmodel. It wasn't long before she'd gotten me into the gym. I was never into working out; I preferred to play sports, though I had slacked off for quite a while before all this. But she had the carrot, and I had the stick. I'd have done just about anything she asked me to, and going to the gym with her and exercising while she was wearing tights and sweating a lot was not much of a sacrifice. Time and time again, it also crossed my mind that I'd better keep my eye on her, so I did. She wasn't a movie star, and I've never dated a movie star, but I imagine this was pretty much the same thing. Strangers were coming up to us to comment on how good she looked or simply pointing and whispering as they went by—it was constant.

Things had been somewhat bleak, tawdry, and disappointing in the period before I met her, and so… just to reiterate and emphasize, I wasn't pretending. I was really in it, perceiving the beauty of life. Good mood, smiling for no reason, enjoying the sweet and simple things of life, all that kinda stuff I'd become so very cynical about; I believed, no bullcrap.

Gradually, she stayed over more and more until we both realized that she had moved in with me for all intents and purposes. First, it was just hanging out. Then she started to keep some of her things at my place. Then, eventually, when her lease was running out, I asked her to move in, and she did it all in one day while I was at work. Wow, what a burst of energy there was around that! People talk about all that force-of-nature stuff around some astounding person they know. That was all true about Bianca, while she was planning to move into my house.

Nor was it long after that our initial discussions about marriage turned into conversations about where and when it would take place and who we would like to invite. Our betrothal quickly became a foregone conclusion.

She was particularly energetic and positive when it came to her product. Her smile was radiant, and she lit up when she told me about her company and its massive success. She told me our company would be worth tens of millions once we sold it, and quite a few corporate entities were already interested in buying it. She began urging me to take a position with the company, so I did. I drew up an agreement and became a 40% shareholder. The 40% was her idea, cleverly assuring me I would be the senior stockholder and that she and I would own 70% together.

For the first time in my life, I became excited about being in business with Bianca. Daydreams of a leisurely retirement from the daily grind of litigation pervaded my thoughts. I'd begun to take the Biotrimus product, too. Bianca sang its praises day and night and took them herself. It was just another facet of all this that became just a matter of time. I was working out regularly and shedding pounds. The pills energized my workouts, but they made me feel jittery, too. I didn't know what to make of that part of it, so, as we did, I kept going.

Every morning, I'd pop the pills in my mouth before even drinking my most important first coffee of the day. If I took the pills any time after 9 a.m., they were so powerful I could not sleep much that night. I think we can safely say there was an upside to this, but as I probably should have known, there might also be a disastrous downside… Bianca didn't sleep much either, so there was plenty of time to stay up and talk and make love till the wee hours. Another big check mark for the upside, I mentally chuckled. And talk and screw and talk and make love and sleep and talk and make magic. Check again!

Aside from the explicitly embarrassing aspects of being the victim of con artists, I can't tell you how ashamed I am of having become obsessed with working out. I never liked the weight room in high school and college, and never after that. I'd always played sports to stay in shape. Tennis, baseball, softball, surfing: it was enough, and I thought better. As mentioned, I'd left all that behind. I convinced myself at some point that I was too busy. Always time for love, though.

I'd also changed my eating habits. That is, I'd stopped eating in the daytime. The goddamn pills suppressed hunger. In not too long a while, I started looking kinda gaunt. My skin became loose because of the rapid fat loss. That said, I continued to take the pills.

And always, always, as I came to understand, when you're dating such a violently pretty woman, that ever-alerting fear was lurking around like the men and the women who embody the idea that some better looking, richer, more fun guy or gal could swoop down and steal her away from me in a moment. My walking-on-air phase had deflated to the degree that suddenly, I wasn't so charming or exciting. Suddenly, I could hear them wondering, "What's this vision doing with *that* guy?"

CHAPTER 3

A Large Dose

Then, my relationship with Bianca changed in the blink of an eye. She asked more often about more money for the company and promised they were on the brink of getting funding from a bank or an investor. I'd become relatively wealthy before all this and primarily hoarded money away in securities. I've always been a hard worker, and I was good enough at it and had the position to do very well. I expensed so much of my life that I'd developed an impressive portfolio. I was certainly no idiot when it came to investment. Yet, there she was, insisting that I allow John to handle the funding aspect of the business since I had the contacts and was the business manager. You bet I agreed. I was her doggy, and she had a-a-a-a-all the bones.

When I was away from her long enough, I would, of course, see the trouble ahead. I kept coming back to the argument that my security would be our engagement instead of my 40%, so I wanted to lock down the deal. I went out and bought a $25,000 engagement ring with a 14-carat diamond rock, took Bianca up to The Post Ranch Inn for a weekend in heaven, and proposed to her during a Saturday evening sunset in our luxurious honeymoon suite. Her saying yes was, as I understood it at the time, the grandest moment of my life! The dreamlike events of dinner and lovemaking that happened after added up to the most important day of my life. I was back in that Bianca-awe-inspired state of bliss described above.

Almost immediately after that weekend, I became complacent about being a lawyer. Based on John's glimmering projections, I spent more and more time speculating about what our lives would be like once we got that rich. We weren't talking about a few million bucks. We were about to become a multi-hundred-million-dollar and billion-dollar empire. Or so they promised. Why should I care about my job? Sure, the firm is the family business, but so what? Soon, I wouldn't have to work at all unless I wanted to.

And Bianca kept filling my head with these fantasies. Oh, she was good. We were about to enjoy a gigantic passive income based on the fruits of their labor and my cunning intellect, support, and love. Once the funding came in, we could expand both production and marketing, which was apparently the Golden Goose scenario that those apparent buyers were waiting to see. I was so whipped at that point that she could've told me the Earth was flat, and I would've believed it. We sold the pills to some influential retailers and on the Internet. This next financing phase would allow us to do a new infomercial on the pill, with Bianca as the spokesmodel. They just needed a little in-between money to push through till the big funds came in. Using my house as collateral—plenty of equity there—I took out a loan.

CHAPTER 4

Danger, Will Robinson, Danger!

Then, the unraveling began in no uncertain terms. I arrived at my office late one morning, as I'd been doing for quite a while at that point, after I'd started dating Bianca. Obviously, if you cut your hours, you cut your billable hours, and so, yes, my billing had suffered significantly. Before all this, I basically lived at the office and worked day and night. Previously, the firm basically enslaved me, so I figured I'd just kick back a bit, waiting for my ship to come in.

As I walked in, a somber, uneasy feeling was in the air. Everyone I looked at tried not to catch my eye. I would describe the look on their faces as mortified but trying to hide it. It reminded me of that scene from *Wall Street* when Bud Fox walks into the office, and no one can make eye contact because the SEC is there to arrest him. As I walked by, the junior partners made eye contact with me from behind the conference room glass. They did not look happy. One of them pointed in the direction I was already going and mouthed the words, "Go see your father."

A flash of adrenaline ran through me as I thought something had happened to my Mom. The furthest thing from my mind was a problem with work. Sure, I'd put in less time, but I had also paid my dues. All the other partners worked flex time when it suited them, and it was fine if they had the book of business and billed enough hours.

I walked into my father's office, and the two other major partners were there with him, waiting for me. I asked, "What's going on?" My father had this authoritative thing that he did with his voice that worked like a charm in court. I called it the *Zeus* voice. With a Zeus-like voice, he told me, rather commanded me to sit down. Obediently, I fell into the tufted, red leather chair that would not soften the impact of this fall from grace. My father was deadly serious as he handed me a class-action suit, alleging that these miracle pills I had been taking caused heart palpitations, seizures, and neurological damage. Some users had suffered cardiac arrest and even heart attacks. I was a named defendant, and Oy Vey, so was the law firm. I cannot even relate to you the overwhelming fear and anxiety that came over me. Dizzy, room spinning, I thought I was about to pass out. Worse yet, Edgar Romero, the famously bellicose and bespectacled plaintiff's attorney, had filed the matter. A real character, as they say, who was notorious for throwing around his substantial ego and weight, respectively, literally and figuratively, taking advantage of a system he knew and understood far too well, time and time again.

The partners were so upset because they had every right to be. I had committed a cardinal sin amongst partners at a law firm. I'd lied by omitting facts my partners needed to know. Here are just some of my lies of omission: I had not bothered to tell anyone that I was General Counsel, which made me the agent for service, which meant the complaint came to me. Oops. Nor had I mentioned the extent of my involvement in Biotrimus.

Frankly, I hadn't mentioned my involvement at all. Quadruple oops. This was one of my dopey self-rationalizations. I'd convinced myself it wasn't necessary since I didn't expect to be working too long after we hit it big. I know it sounds stupid to me, too. I'm sure I folded it into the idea of empowerment at the time. I'm also sure my self-empowerment included the kind of greed that had no intention of sharing any of the windfalls with my loving partners. I resented ALL the partners, including my father. They were greedy, rigid, and often evil men who had trained me to be just like them.

Wait, it still gets worse. I had pledged my partnership equity in the law firm as collateral for some of the loans I'd taken out on the company. Is that not bad enough for you? We'd neglected to buy the appropriate insurance coverage for Biotrimus, as only two carriers would take on this type of risk. They were nonadmitted carriers, at a very high premium, with substantial self-insured retention as well, meaning that we had to spend $100,000 on defense fees and litigation costs before the insurance would kick in. So, I made the executive decision to screw it. Arrogantly, I'd presumed my own father's firm, where I was a partner, would support me if anything ever went this wrong. Boy, was I mistaken.

Not surprisingly, in retrospect, there was also a weird feeling in the air at home that morning. Bianca had left in a rush, saying she would be in heavy-duty meetings with John all day. She was rushing to get out, but I thought she was just ramping up for a big day of work. Ultimately, I guess that was so. I was still half-asleep in bed when she slipped out the door.

As soon as I could get out of the meeting, I desperately tried to contact Bianca and John to break the news. I remember having the romantic thought of, "Well, at least we're in it together." She would provide comfort and solace, and I would be her knight in shining armor. Until now, my old alert system has finally gone off again, and it was now full tilt. "Where have ya' been?" I wondered. All the ulterior motives and subterfuge came rushing in all at once. Back when I'd begun to think twice about Bianca, I'd end up telling myself I was being paranoid and sabotaging the best thing that ever happened to me. Seriously, Dale, I'd tell myself, you need to deal with these trust issues and leave it at that.

My many attempts at reaching Bianca and John through email, text, and voicemail amounted to nil. She had previously always made herself available to me and made sure to get back to me even if she was in a meeting—not this time.

Then a call came in. Something was very wrong, and I had to get home. I was relieved to have the excuse to leave. I drove back insanely fast without regard for the rules of the road; it was irresponsible, even under the circumstances. As so very many, very crazy thoughts were racing through my head, I suddenly realized that they were very crazy thoughts, and I couldn't help but consider that I was going insane.

I pulled up to the house, walked in the door, and immediately knew that my worst nightmare had become reality. Bianca had taken all her stuff. She'd even taken some of *my* stuff! "What the fuck!" All those months, I'd thought that I finally had a good woman by my side and that we could get through anything together.

Idiotically, I was worried about Bianca and how she would take the news of the complaint. I guess I was in a state of shock. I'd been feeling somewhat nauseous and dizzy all day since my meeting with Lucifer, uh, my Dad, and the partners. Standing in the doorway, these symptoms hit home. I stumbled over the end table and the carpet, using my arms as stilts of sorts to keep myself from passing out on the floor. I wanted to pass out on the couch! The nausea and spinning head were not kind.

My world cracked… I curled up in a fetal position to ride it out, moaning out loud.

As usual, I'd taken a couple of Biotrimus pills (with a macchiato from the French café on the way to the office) in the morning since I'd felt lethargic, and they had kicked in. There, on my beautiful sofa, I was experiencing some of the same symptoms the plaintiffs had alleged in the complaint—lightheaded, dazed, heart racing out of control. Nausea led to dry heaves and shakes.

After, I guess, several hours of this (I have no idea how long it might have been), I managed to stabilize somewhat before falling asleep, only to be awakened by vicious nightmares. My last thoughts that night were in the realm of the following: just a short time ago, I was on top of the world. With that girl on my arm and our future together, along with the gig I already had, I thought I was one of the coolest attorneys in LA—maybe the coolest. Today, it all turned from a dream to a nightmare. Not to mention fraud. Not in a legal sense, of course, but… and then I got confused between the fraud of my relationship and goddam betrothal and this highly questionable business venture, equivocating idiotically with myself before giving up.

Finally, I merely wished for a better life—a good one—and to be out of this suffering. And then I fell into the Bliss of Sleep.

CHAPTER 5

Buddha Dream

Unaware that I was now asleep, I was also unaware that I was in a dream. The physical world, for lack of a better term, seemed so real until this moment. However, this murky, intensely painful, scary dream world seemed surreal, which I don't mean dreamy. I mean, intensely and extraordinarily real.

In the wee hours, straddling late night and early morning from the darkness, a golden orb of light appeared, moving ever closer into my awareness. Generally, something moving toward me in a dream would have probably freaked me out. However, because of the serenity of the scene, it was different. As it moved closer, I became calmer. The gold orb came so close that it filled my vision completely until I distinctly heard a very light pop, like the sound of a soap bubble popping in a kid's game, followed by the realization that I was no longer alone.

I was now within the rays of the golden orb. Floating in the air in front of me was a Buddha-like being just a few feet away. I do not remember ever feeling this calm, nor do I remember ever feeling so infinitely at home. Was this Gautama—aka Siddhartha Gautama—aka Buddha? *The Buddha?* I could not manage to ask. What I understood about the situation was that before I sat at A Golden Buddha in A Golden Space, I was completely calm for the first time in as long as I can remember. There was no weight or tension in my body. What I would describe as a wave of love without beginning or ending passed through me in a form that I perceived to include the following words:

"Dale… the life you just wished for is possible. To attain this state of being, you must simply let it in and let it fill you."

The Buddha continued: "Now that we have heard your sincere cry for help, the first step is to accept that this physical world you think you are alive in is merely an illusion. It is an illusion within your mind. Though this is a simple concept, it is not all that easy to grasp fully. Take my hand."

I suddenly experienced a wave of fear and anger, which was just as suddenly vanquished by the wave of love beaming from his face and throat and heart and the beautiful form of his open hand. I took his hand; a moment I cannot fully describe but will simply relate that I lost all sense of time passing. There was no time for it. Somewhere in there, however, I asked, "Why are you helping me?"

The Buddha smiled gracefully and, in a tone unlike any other, he shared: "Because you asked sincerely. Because your cry was sincere." He then elaborated on what felt like another wave of love. I pondered what was happening. I was now thinking in a dream, which was an odd realization, as I was much more awake than I had ever remembered. I could not sufficiently characterize it nor even begin to quote it since it did not seem like spoken language, but it was something about being moved by my sincere desire to get out of the misery I found myself in and that his compassionate nature allowed him to reach out when genuine cries for help warranted it.

All my realizations and experiences were blowing together in this surreal montage. Toward the end of the sequence, he concluded with something very much in tune with: "Dale, you can get out of suffering," and we sat with that together for a while, allowing me the chance to take it all in fully.

He then continued, "Please understand that your identification with the world you think is around you is what is causing you all this pain. So long as you believe that that world is a reality when it is positively illusory, you can *never* escape that prison because the *you* who knows your weaknesses so well has built this prison specifically for the *you* who is struggling so hard to survive and even thrive there, and you will never be free. In that ego mode of survival, with all the emotions and beliefs of that world swirling around you, penetrating your very soul, in time, one becomes lost to the peace at the center of who we categorically are—lost to the presence of our true nature."

I could feel something inside me was changing. That lit, timeless, spaceless impression had continued throughout. It occurred to me I had been reactive and defensive all my life, even on offense, if that makes any sense. So many times, day after day, I filled my life with high hopes of glorious outcomes, be they financial, work-related, or in my personal life. Yet, even when I succeeded in the task or the accomplishment, it was never accompanied by the dream-come-true feeling it was supposed to come along with.

Yes, there were slaps on the back, glad-handing, and financial and, shall we call them, personal rewards? I was certainly foolish enough to believe all my dreams were coming true because of Bianca, though that has no place on anyone's list of accomplishments. Yet, reflecting on my adventures thus far in life in the now of this dream, there was most often simply a sense of relief that—whatever it was over—and I hadn't blown it. And, sometimes, I felt bitter, realizing that my success was overrated.

This feeling of lightness through and through was gaining momentum. I felt something wash through from my core to my currently hard-to-decipher periphery that hit my consciousness in the form of the words: *I'm free.* I was now feeling the strength to be proactive about what was being set before me. And along with this feeling came perhaps the sweetest kind of hope. Supposedly, I could somehow maintain the humility to set aside all that had built up my ego, ultimately breaking me. In that case, I might just be able to bring the deeper reality that the Buddha was so eloquently transmitting to me into my life.

He let go of my hand, yet was still there with me. I humbly asked another question: "How do I change it?"

The Buddha beamed compassion: "So simple. So very simple, but not easy! I will teach you **The Three Priceless Techniques.** The more one applies these *techniques* in daily life, the easier they become, and the less stressful one's life will be. The results will be peace, understanding, an awareness of the meaning of life and consciousness, and the exquisite pleasure of helping those around you with love."

The Buddha continued: "Understand, these *techniques* will do far more than help you work out the problems of your life. Your correct actions will be tantamount to magnetic fields, influencing others to do the same. As more people do them, you and others will transform the world into a giant *Buddha Field.*"

"What's a *Buddha Field?*" I asked.

"A very fine question, my dear, since it is the subject of our next lesson. For now, consider this: to understand where we are going, we must first understand where we have been." His hypnotic gaze took my breath away. He nodded so infinitely that there was nothing else to say, though he did have one syllable to add. He held his forefinger aloft, still nodding in that heavenly way, and said, "Yes."

CHAPTER 6

The Realization

When I came to, I was in a fog on the beach. Groggily, I recalled having a dream involving a Buddha of sorts, a profound vision, perhaps. I saw puzzles in my mind and loose pieces that needed to take their place. Once I'd put it all together, the finished puzzle told the story. It was a nasty story. The thought of her insisting I texted her when I left home for the office that morning encapsulates the larger story at hand. As I lay there immobilized, it became clear as a bell: the Liberty Bell landing on me from some great height, crack and all, and BONG, BONG, BONG! The whole affair had been part of an elaborate scam.

Was it PT Barnum or WC Fields who said: "There's a sucker born every minute?" Whoever said it, they were right, and I was the sucker.

How humiliating to review my romantic notion that the two of us were in it together. Well, I guess she was in it, along with John. Upon reflection, it makes sense that they were lovers throughout this entire fiasco. They were always together and traveled together for business. Why should I think twice about it, right? He was gay, right? Still in the closet, right? Our little secret, right? Wrong.

They knew the lawsuit was coming—filed a day before it landed on dear old Dad's desk. I later discovered that Romero had written a letter to Biotrimus that I never saw and, get this, Bianca and John ignored it. I'm a lawyer, goddammit! Not just any lawyer, but a partner at an in-the-game LA firm with resources! I guess they surreptitiously removed me from the contact list and then tracked the county court's website. Seeing the lawsuit filed, they jumped ship.

On my walk back from the beach, caffeine racing through my mind, then pacing around the living room, I went through all of it. Then, another terrible rush coursed through my brain, body, and blood. Dizzy and sick to my stomach once again, my vision blurred. For a second, I remembered the Buddha dream. I didn't make it to the couch. My legs went out from under me, and I fell to the floor. All at once, decades of anger and resentment blew open all the doors of all my previous hang-ups.

For what seemed like hours, I had one tantrum after another, like a baby going to town, no holds barred. I pounded the floor, wept, and screamed. I'd get to a point where I thought I'd gotten it all out, and another blast would blow through all over again. At some point, the dust settled. I sat there in shock. What a schmuck I'd been! I went over the last ten months again and simply couldn't believe I missed sign after sign. How could I have let these mediocre con artists burn me like this?! I felt so stupid, played for a fool. It rolled around in my head like that for hours until I finally fell asleep–that Bliss of Sleep—I don't know when. I'm almost embarrassed to relate the insipid nightmare I had. Bianca was a witch, a very hot witch—riding her broom, chasing me down, spear in hand, trying to get a clean shot at me. Meanwhile, I'm helplessly free-falling into some mythic abyss, naked as the day I was born.

She was looking to skewer me with that spear, then bring me home and roast me over an open fire. The dream did not resolve itself. I woke up in a cold sweat, my heart racing, breathing hard, overwhelmed, and confused. The rejection was unbearable. It hadn't been long since that best night and day of my life. Now, the worst day and night of my life had wiped that most beautiful experience away forever. A surfer friend in Malibu once said, "There's a Led Zeppelin song for every human emotion and some human emotions that haven't been invented yet. For me: Cue *Good Times, Bad Times* by Led Zeppelin. Or maybe *Dazed and Confused*:

Been dazed and confused for so long, it's not true.
Wanted a woman, never bargained for you.
Lots of people talkin', few of them know
Soul of a woman was created below, yeah![3]

[3] "Dazed and Confused," Led Zeppelin (Led Zeppelin I), 1969. These lines are excerpted from the song; all rights to the original composition and recording are reserved by the artists and distributors.

CHAPTER 7

Depression Sets In

Though not formally diagnosed, I was having a nervous breakdown. I couldn't work (even though I was unemployed), couldn't leave the house, and couldn't function at all. I was so humiliated by this real-life nightmare. Forget about Bianca, the witch in my dream. This was far worse.

Speaking of nightmares, they became a big part of the problem. I've read that shark attack victims say the worst part of their experience is the nightmares and PTSD, or in this case, Post Traumatic Shark Disorder, because now they know and fear what's coming. They fed my insomnia—every night for a good while, an hour or two sleep tops. I'd fade away well after midnight and wake up a half-hour later drenched in sweat, anxious, sometimes trembling, with vague memories of a handful of recurring dreams. I'd calm myself down to a degree, maybe doze off again after a while, then the same result: soaking wet and terrified, then simmering down to paralyzing depression. That was my life. I resolved to stop taking the Biotrimus, as you might imagine. No problem going cold turkey after all I'd been through and reading that damning complaint.

In the morning, I'd go over to a local doughnut shop for breakfast. Coffee and doughnuts, or maybe a pastry, probably wasn't the best thing for me, but there was zero chance of me preparing something for myself, so I'd drag myself over there each morning just to get something inside me. The sugar and the caffeine would have to suffice for now.

Bad breakfasts aside, I didn't eat much at all. When I did, it was either delivery from a local restaurant or canned food and Top Ramen. I'd filled a shopping cart in the middle of the night soon after that fateful day. You'd be surprised how satisfying SpaghettiOs can be straight out of the can without heating them up, especially when you're losing your mind.

I've read my share of mental illness. I was a textbook, self-diagnosed, classic case of depression. The very few who knew and saw me agreed wholeheartedly. Articles in our pop culture flood the market, so it's hard to avoid. Taking care of oneself doesn't make it into many playbooks, but I was just too terrified to leave the house. The pain I was in, the shame, the humiliation, it was more than I could handle.

It became clear rather quickly that, aside from my brother Todd and my secretary Sherry, no one cared about me, including my father. Unfortunately, my Mom did what my Dad did, and she didn't talk to me either. Sherry was my only contact with the life I had known up to the moment of my disintegration. Or maybe she was just doing her job; I dunno. I had enough going on in my head without having to analyze this, too. If, in fact, Sherry staying in touch with me was merely her functioning as an employee of the firm, that brief list of two just got cut in half, leaving only Todd.

The days and nights blurred together. Time became an otherworldly phenomenon. One night, laid out in bed, desperate for sleep, I looked up at the ceiling. Those apparently magic words went through my mind. I don't really pray, but this was a sincere, fervent prayer: "Please help me!"

CHAPTER 8

The Review of Early Life

Seemingly from a *Buddha Balcony*… or, I don't know, elevated somehow, the Buddha and I looked down on a courtroom. Over the years, I have seen the inside of a legal courtroom so many times. It was always mixed emotions from memories of kicking ass and cremating my opponent. Justice aside, as long as I won, it was all good. I had many flashbacks of getting my ass handed to me when someone had the balls to stand up to our mega-firm, and the Judge saw right through my BS.

However, as I looked around this time, I was amazed to see everyone there was *me*. I was the judge, plaintiff, plaintiff's counsel, defendant, and defense counsel, all the jurors, the clerk, the court reporter, the bailiff, and everyone in the gallery; they were all me. As you might imagine, I was astonished and paid even closer attention, yet the chatter of all of them—or all of me—added to an indecipherable wave of sound.

Seeing everyone as me was more than earth-shattering. It was strange to make this realization during a dream. It was a real trip, to say the least, seeing myself as all the players in the dynamics of a courtroom.

Looking through the eyes of yours truly hanging out with the Buddha, the judge used his gavel to bring the court to order, and the strange wave of sound faded to silence. The judge and the plaintiff's counsel traded a few phrases that were also indecipherable to me. Then, the Court went dark, and a film began: moving images of a small boy with his older brother, which became clear that it was Todd and me.

Ever since I could walk, and probably even before that, I followed Todd around. I imitated and worshiped him. My idol was about two-and-a-half years older than me, and older brothers aren't always so kind to their younger siblings, but we had a wonderful bond between us. It had been so natural, so sweet and easy, and the film images reflected that. That good feeling is still in my memory and soul and in stark contrast to the conservative family and community we grew up in. Yes, we grew up in Los Angeles in the '60s and '70s. But, no, my folks were definitely not hippies.

We were both boomers. I was one of the last, born in May 1964, and Todd had come before me in November of '61, both with silver spoons in our mouths. Our parents, Patricia and Tate Owen, Jr., were already quite successful. We lived on a hill overlooking Santa Monica Bay: a long walk, a quick bike ride, a dangerous skateboard run, or a brief drive to the prestigious country club at the beach that was the center of our lives and cemented our social status.

We didn't want to just *keep up with the Joneses;* we were the Joneses!

Originally named Tate III, Todd no longer went by that name for reasons you will come to understand. For as long as I can remember, even over the past several years since he'd separated himself from the family, Todd has been my idol.

The early childhood scenes cut into me wonderfully. In watching these scenes, all brought back from the passage of time itself, I could see Tate's brotherly love for me. Even as a little kid, he so clearly wanted to protect me. It struck me to the core, and I wept in a way that felt like I'd let go of something I'd been holding onto for too long. Though I couldn't tell you what it was, had it not been from this *Buddha Balcony* perspective, I wouldn't have seen this aspect of our relationship so

clearly. One scene after another, like that, and as we got older. I was being reminded there was such a sense of peace between my brother and me and that I had known nowhere else; a genuinely beautiful thing between us.

Then, a disjointed, confusing montage of scenes around my parents' meeting. I guess it wasn't very pleasant of me to say, but the scenes I saw made it terribly clear that their purpose in life was to become successful, make as much money, and have as much prestige as possible. My Mom became the featured player in the first part of this montage.

Images of Patricia Anne Wainwright flashed as a child and teenager who grew up on a ranch outside Kansas City, Missouri. She was the first woman on that side of the family to go to college, somehow deciding she wanted to live in San Diego in high school and get herself into USD. It was not unimpressive. Maybe she thought she should go to California because, in that landlocked part of Missouri, she appeared to be the classic *California Girl.* Bubbly, in a good way, troublingly pretty, surprisingly smart, and blessed with the blond hair and bright blue eyes that have been part of the California Dream ever since the first Europeans got here.

Then, there are shots of Mom meeting Dad while doing a summer stint in LA at a local TV station. Like so many pretty girls who made their way out west, she dreamed of being on TV. What better place to get discovered than at a TV station?

Then, some images of my father and his father, my Dad home from Stanford for the summer after his first year of law school and clerking at The Law Offices of Tate J. Owen. Pat and Tate met, and apparently, sparks flew. They fell madly in love and were engaged by Christmas. Dad flew back to Missouri with Mom to spend a traditional holiday with her and pay his respects to the Wainwrights, asking Patty's Dad, Henry, for her hand in marriage. Tate seemed to be pleasant, and all the boxes checked off, so Henry graciously agreed and wished them luck, and days later, threw an engagement party that was the talk of the town.

I looked over to the Buddha, who was already looking at me. I didn't see his lips move, yet I could have sworn I heard him say, "Do you perceive the patterns here?" I turned back to the screen attentively.

Now, it was another scene from my childhood. Blue Sparrow Elementary School paved the way for Saint Anton's High. I was doing what was expected of me, and Todd was not, much to our parents' chagrin, frustration, and embarrassment.

We were slightly rambunctious, fun-loving kids growing up, and pretty normal. Up against that upper-crust setting, though, normal kids might have seemed problematic. I can assure you, in that time and place, we weren't the only ones. We were given tennis rackets, golf clubs, and lessons on how to use them at an early age, as were most of our peers. Things rolled along like that for a while. Then came a time when I continued to do what was expected of me in our parents' circle, but Todd could not. He couldn't focus on playing sports, on anything he was studying in school, or on anything else. By the time I graduated Magna Cum Laude and had been captain of the tennis team at St. Anton's, my ride through a prestigious undergrad program and a venerable law school was fixed in place. All I had to do was do what I was told. Meanwhile, Todd was in the process of disappearing.

We lived about four miles up the hill from the beach. It was about a two-mile downhill ride on the bike or skateboard before the road flattened out, which was fun. Yes, here we have some images of Todd sailing down the hill with me. Since, according to our parents, the public beaches in Santa Monica didn't have *the right kind of people,* we were discouraged from going there and absolutely forbidden to go alone, so we went together. With friends and families, we could come and go from the club, though, and our love of the beach grew stronger every year on both sides of the fence: fine old memories at the beach. When we got older, it turned into an intense connection to the ocean.

The proximity to the water provided more than a respite from the heat waves that hit LA from time to time. It calmed our minds and eased the pressure at home—old pictures of the bay around sunset.

The concluding images begin with Tate Jr. He was a powerful, inquisitive father figure, along with being a driven, ambitious attorney, and believe me, none of that added up to some kind of cool '60s LA lawyer Dad. He had his moments, but he was tough on us, silver spoons and all.

I've heard plenty about what a hard man his father had been, but Tate Sr. (we called him *Poppa*—with an air of eccentricity) was sweet as pie with Todd and me, though I do remember him slamming a lot of doors. He started his own firm and kept control of it, eventually going into partnership only with his son (our dear old Dad), Tate Jr., many years later.

Thus giving birth to the firm's legal name, "Owen and Owen, LLP," which it has remained despite subsequent partners and all ever since. Some bright images of the two of them together at the office faded into images of the two of them at our house. My mother was serving them, very young and beautiful, all very pleasantly in the sunshine, which further faded into images of the sounds of our parents fighting while Todd and I were supposed to be asleep.

Didn't they know we could hear them through the door? It happened all the time.

Suddenly, the screen went black, and the courtroom lights lit up. I wasn't everybody anymore. I didn't even have anything to do with the trial. Simply a man sitting in the gallery. Nor was I sitting in the elevated space with the Buddha. I was just that man in the audience in the courtroom, sitting and watching the proceedings.

I did recognize one person in the courtroom—the bailiff. Todd was the bailiff. He tipped his cap to me and flashed me that sly smile of his.

The judge said: "Mr. Walker?"

Walker began: "If it pleases the court, your honor, there's more."

The judge said: "Let's have lunch and come back at 1:30 p.m. sharp, counsel," and banged his gavel once to adjourn us, which woke me up, I must say, incredibly refreshed. I hadn't felt that good for quite a while, and I remember feeling very easy, sleepy in that normal way on my way to the commode in the middle of the night, then going back to bed and falling asleep without a hitch, as if everything was just fine. As dreamlike as the dream itself. In fact, I may have dreamed it. I can't be sure. What I do remember is that when I looked at my clock before I closed my eyes, it was 3:32 a.m.

CHAPTER 9

A Review of My Adolescent Days

I folded right back into the dream, though this time in the defendant's chair, wearing tennis clothes. There was a strange courtroom murmur, not like anything I had heard before in court, but a distorted concept of that courtroom, a digital whir imitation. My lawyer was talking to me, reassuringly tapping my hand repeatedly with a few fingers, but what he was saying was just part of the whir. The judge walked evenly from his chambers to the bench, took his seat, banged the gavel gently a few times, and said: "Proceed, Mr. Walker."

"More film, your honor."

"Proceed," and the lights went out again.

As a young man, I was girl-shy. What made it worse was the *you're-so-cute!* stuff. Trust me, girls, no teenage boy wants to hear that, especially if you're going to go off and screw the quarterback who, in my day, anyway, split a 'lude with you to open you up nice and easy. Or worse. It confused me.

So, we see some scenes of me as a teenager trying to talk to girls and them telling me I'm nice or cute in that put-you-off way. I dunno; it messed me up, and in the dream, it made me remember that feeling: that it made me freeze and turn into this timid, quiet, polite kid, acting the way I would around adults instead of other boys. I didn't make waves, so when it came to adults and girls, I was liked by almost everyone. It just never got me any tail. I got cornered into that mode through high school. I had a few close friends I did school stuff and sports with, but I didn't roam far from that safety zone.

That all changed in the second semester of my senior year when I finally noticed Laurie Masters. Seeing her up there on the screen hit me right in the throat. She lived a few blocks down the street, and our families knew each other from the beach club. Her father was supposed to be some kind of brilliant scientist and her Mom a screenwriter—who looked damn good in a bathing suit, I might add, but I'd never noticed Laurie as more than another girl at school and the club until she, well, wasn't just a girl anymore.

Not that I could say anything to her. I was Mr. Don't-Make-Waves, remember?

The only reason I could finally manage to break through with her was how elated I was that Stanford had accepted me. I had the confidence to walk up to her at a friend's keg party and start talking to her. Her parents were out of town, so I thought the time was right. After ten minutes or so, I remember thinking I wasn't that kid who's so nice to parents and girls; I was acting more like the *me* who hangs out with his friends. Soon followed by the goofy thought of, wow, I'm really doing this!

I walked her home, and we talked some more. She told me it was hard having such impressive parents and that she always felt in their shadow. We walked and talked for just a few blocks that I wish had been a hundred—balmy, starlit, crescent moon night in a dream. We'd been bumping arms comfortably as we walked, and, at one point, I reached my hand out gently for hers, and she took it. It was euphoric.

We got to her house, slipped into the backyard, and walked to the back of the property. We sat down on the grass by the studio back there and talked in the dark some more. The lawn was wet, although we didn't care. After a while, I just had to kiss her again, and she kissed back. Excited and frightened, it felt too good to stop, but after a while, we did. It had gotten too deep for both of us and was very late, so we agreed to date and never looked back from there.

We talked for the rest of the night. She seemed interested in me and listened. I hadn't ever looked directly into a girl's eyes for an extended period before and been myself as we spoke. I was probably just blathering on about going to Stanford, but she was there with me. As the party was coming to an end and almost everybody had gone home or elsewhere, we started to kiss and then didn't stop. I was nearly 18 and had never had a real kiss before. Sure, spin-the-bottle, drunk, but this was the first real thing.

Laurie and I became increasingly close as the school year ended. We spent all our free time together. At that moment in life, at the end of high school, I was one of the lucky ones. I had a girlfriend who became my best friend. We taught each other how to have sex and figured out ways to get away with it without rattling our parents' preconceived notions about us. If you'd asked me when we graduated, I would have told you I was going to marry that girl one day. If only I had been that smart.

As Laurie and I spent more time together, I spent less time with my family and Todd. He was happy for me, but he was drifting away. High school was a breeze since Stanford had already accepted me, and I had nothing more to do than pass my classes. I wasn't offered a tennis scholarship or even a position on the team. Instead, I was playing a lot of tennis, hoping to make it heroically as a walk-on. Between Laurie, school, and tennis, I could avoid most of the angst and discomfort of being a teenager at home.

There was also a bit of a comedy going on that spring and summer between my father and me. I'd gotten pretty good at tennis by then. Everyone at the club knew it and wanted their shot. Dad would ask me to take it easy on certain important members and other kids: let this or that one somehow beat me, or at least let them think they could keep up with me—but I just didn't have it in me to let up or lose on purpose.

He'd try to explain to me that this or that match on this or that day could be worth hundreds of thousands or maybe even millions of dollars to him, but he could never get through to me. They all took their shot at me, and they all went down in flames, a few of them badly injured. There it was: that look of dismay and disappointment on my father's face for winning.

He could never understand why I didn't understand, but he made me that way. That look of his is burned into my soul.

So, it wasn't 1967; my summer of love was 1983. Laurie wasn't just my girlfriend; she was my closest friend and confidant, and I was hers. Maybe the Beach Boys also have a song for every human experience: *Wouldn't It Be Nice* or *All Summer Long* would work for Laurie and me. Our parents were all well above reproach, and, lucky for us, they didn't socialize with each other. Both sides simply approved and let us do what we wanted so long as we didn't get into any trouble, which was one of my few areas of expertise. It felt so good to be with her. I really thought we were going to spend our lives together. The last images of this sequence on the screen are of Laurie and me sitting on the beach, talking and laughing together around sunset, the sound of the shore break washing through it. Our adolescent existence was pure magic. I felt my heart break right then in the dream of watching it.

I looked over at the Buddha for comfort, and he maintained his demeanor of peace and tranquility. I thought to myself in the dream: Wasn't he going to comfort me? Wasn't he supposed to make it all better? Should there even be consideration of comfort as this whole thing is an illusion while I'm having a dream watching a memory, which was also like a dream? Wow, I just asked myself a lot of questions. I laughed to myself. I hope I get the answers.

CHAPTER 10

College and Law School Review

I moved to Palo Alto and lived in a dorm during my first year at Stanford, while Laurie remained in LA for her last year of high school. We talked on the phone pretty much every day, sometimes twice a day. Remember, this was a time when only grounded landlines existed. I couldn't just take my phone out of my pocket and call or text. The phone company billed differently in those days, too. All those calls led to ridiculously high phone bills, but frankly, with our folks paying our way, I don't remember thinking much about it.

Up on the screen, we see a split-screen of Laurie and me talking on the phone and some shots of us back in LA when I would come down to visit, which was as often as possible.

Drinking and smoking weed, or pot, as we usually referred to it back then, made bonding with my new college pals easy. It was normal. I made it to the tennis team—barely, as a walk-on—and I was proud of that, but I had to deal with the reality that I was the worst singles player on the team. In competition, I mostly played doubles and felt lucky to have John Dinsdale as my partner. He was from Orinda, a pretty, little swanky town just east of Berkeley, and a damn good player who made me much better. He was tall and lanky with a big serve and was fast to the net when he was serving, while I was not so tall and muscle-bound with solid, consistent groundstrokes, which added up to us being a good team that could win a moderate amount of recognition and borderline collegiate fame. We became best friends pretty quickly and spent a lot of that first year together.

Images passed to and fro of us playing tennis, hanging out, partying, perhaps far too happy, that is, soused, in some of the latter.

Then, there is a broader montage, a rough sketch of the next couple of years. I majored in history, and it seemed funny to me that whoever put this film together intertwined historical images, the Greeks, the Romans, etc., with my story, leading all the way up to that present moment and the Reagan Administration.

I did pretty well as an undergrad, but my grades and LSAT score were not quite good enough to get me into Stanford Law School, much to the chagrin of my father. He got subtly angry about it, barely able to hide his contempt as if I weren't good enough, not so much at me as the fact that his attempts to pull the right strings didn't succeed. He had been an undergrad there and had also gone to law school. Also, Dad was very active in the Alumni Association, donating significant sums of money to the school every year. He felt like my grades were good enough for a legacy, but the powers that be didn't agree, and man, was he *pissed.*

I was, however, accepted at Gould, USC's Law School, which seemed like a stroke of good luck. Laurie and I had continued our long-distance relationship, seeing each other when I could get down to LA, and she came up to Palo Alto once in a while after she'd gotten into UCLA and moved out of her parents' house.

Now that I was moving back to Los Angeles, we thought we could finally have a real-life love affair and were talking about moving in together once I'd settled back into LA. Yet, when I did get back, I was irritable with her and arrogant, too. I guess with the pressure of being a first-year law student, where almost everyone (not everyone) was both intelligent and, really, dangerously ambitious (not everyone), I was too self-absorbed and failed to reconnect with her properly.

My metamorphosis to becoming an asshole attorney was in its infancy.

From the *Buddha Balcony,* we watched my aircraft carrier-sized arrogance on full display. Again, I looked over at the Buddha rather than expecting him to judge me. He still maintained his serenity and loving gaze, even while I was clearly an egotistical ass.

Maybe it was just youth and ignorance; I can't pretend to understand what happened and still don't know to this day why I made myself emotionally unavailable to her. The easy intimacy and beautiful friendship, which still existed while I was up north, somehow vanished when I came back home. Watching myself up on that screen acting indifferently with my first love, perhaps my one true love, just throwing it away like that brought me to tears. Maybe the greatest mistake of my life.

During the winter holiday break, she broke up with me. I will never forget how she wanted to come over after a week of strained discomfort with her. It was just before Christmas, and she wanted to have a little chat. Her eyes glistened with tears as she said, "It just wasn't working out anymore," and that we could be *friends forever* (Jeez, thanks)! I pressed her, dissatisfied with her explanation and justification for our split. After reacting like a jerk and browbeating her to tell me why she wanted to end our blissful union, she told me she didn't know who I was anymore. I knew that in my heart of hearts, and she was right. At the time, however, I was dumb enough to pretend not to care. Inside, my heart fractured deeply, but I just bottled it all up and continued my ambitious path to riches and fame.

Now roll some images of Todd's complete withdrawal from the family on the *Buddha Balcony* screen. Still a young man while I was in law school, as far as the family was concerned, Todd fell off the deep end. Drifting from odd job to odd job, essentially homeless at times, but for the fact that he knew enough people to have places to crash when necessary, our folks continued to bail him out when he was in enough trouble. Sure, the only time they heard from him was when he needed money. What made it even sadder to me was that they funded him not so much out of love, but to avoid the embarrassment of the idea that a son of theirs could become homeless. I regret to say that I also pretty much disowned him and kept him at a safe distance during those years.

I looked over at the Buddha and mentally said to him: "WOW, I just lost the two loves of my life. That hurt! Connection with others is *VERY IMPORTANT*." While his expression didn't change, I swore I saw or possibly imagined a micro-blink of an eye in recognition of my realization.

At the end of my first year at USC Law, after a charade of an interview, I became a Summer Associate at Owen and Owen. It was funny. The firm had a strict *antinepotism policy,* but everyone knew better, especially me. I went through the motions, and they actually staged an interview. When I came aboard, I got to enjoy the advantages of being the Golden Boy. Yes, firms entice young romantic recruits with great seats at ballgames, lunches, and dinners at high-end joints, Bar-B-Qs, and lavish parties, among the important ones on the weekends, all to lure you into the firm. But I was a foregone conclusion, and there was no need for romance or a lure. So, I played along and took full advantage of the fun part of it. As far as work was concerned, I plodded along doing research memorandums and the other tedious tasks that were set in front of me. Typically, this sort of work is supposed to help one get a feel for a firm, but this firm was already in my blood and brain. In addition, no one was going to put up a particularly egregious task for me. It was easy that summer, and I had a ball.

Again, thanks to my Dad, after my second year in law school, my summer job was clerking for Appellate Court Justice Errol Hager for the LA 2nd Division Court of Appeals. Quite a bit more responsibility, and I certainly learned a lot more than my previous summer at Owen & Owen, but also rather mundane as far as the work was concerned. The perks were a dim shadow compared to what I'd had access to the summer before. It was amusing to watch how the easy, well-appointed

sunshine imagery of that first summer turned into a series of depressing, claustrophobic, cold, and dank images, the latter presumably from lousy air conditioning and the drudgery of the work.

However, the intellectual pursuit and seeing my writing and language in an opinion published by Justice Hager was another boost to my increasingly inflated ego.

During the summer after Law School, I entrenched myself in my studies and unilaterally focused on passing the State Bar. I graduated from Gould after cruising through my third year, enjoying the visualization of light at the end of the tunnel. My vanity took quite a hit, though. As I say, I had been single-minded in studying for the Bar. However, on the day of the test, I had such a bad case of test anxiety that I couldn't even think straight and failed the exam. I was used to a certain amount of anxiousness before an exam, but had never experienced anything quite so debilitating as that. Nor did I get the chance to calm down afterward completely.

I tried to console myself by knowing that JFK Jr. failed the New York Bar exam twice before getting it on the third try. John and I weren't alone in failing the bar and joining a list that included Franklin D. Roosevelt and California governors Jerry Brown and Pete Wilson. Antonio Villaraigosa failed the bar *four* times before throwing in the towel, but still became mayor of Los Angeles. The former dean of Stanford Law School, Kathleen Sullivan, failed the bar on her first attempt. So I was in good company, but that wasn't too consoling.

Along with fear and stupidity, I felt relentless pressure from my father and anyone from the firm. Hell, anyone who even knew about it made me uncomfortable. I think those were the first times in my life I was waking up drenched in sweat and panicked. And that laser beam of disappointment from my father was inescapable. I was so humiliated, I didn't socialize or talk to anyone I knew for the next six months: as little as possible became my standard. If I went out, I'd go alone to places no one could recognize me. Thank God I passed on the second try, but I suffered through the waiting period between the test and posting the results! It was like walking around with a knife to my throat. To my brain. To my future.

This time, I could swear that the Buddha looked at me and mentally said, "Do you see how the interactions between you and your father shaped you?" Even if the Buddha didn't say it, I was certainly observing and thinking about it.

CHAPTER 11

The Review of Brother Todd

The screen faded to black after the previous sequence, slowly filling with a light gray fog. Once the screen had become dense with fog, that imagery began to float out into and fill the entire courtroom so that I could see nothing but gray with some kind of backlighting. I felt an absolute calm in that gray for a while, and then the fog began to dissipate in the room and on the screen, and once it had, scenes of my family emerged again. I was back with the Buddha in the elevated space, viewing the courtroom below, and still in the defendant's chair with another me. I felt so light being in the presence of the Buddha once again. There was also the impression that I was being presented with these scenes as a chance to come to terms with and resolve the damage from all the trauma I'd experienced in my life: not just some, but all. The heaviness of the past was somehow being removed from my soul.

It is especially apropos that this particular sequence was coming to me in the form of a movie since my parents, my brother, and I were, for a time, indeed, the picture of the perfect nuclear family. As I view some early, idealized images of the four of us, I wonder what would happen if all the energy that goes into keeping up appearances were refocused on love and compassion instead.

At home, though, as at the office, Dad was a tyrant. If things went his way, he wasn't all that bad, but when they didn't, he didn't have much patience for any of us. We watched scenes of my father's authoritarian behavior. I saw such sadness in my eyes when a small boy was on the receiving end of it and being rendered completely powerless. I looked over to the Buddha for comfort. His eyes effused rays of loving support.

Todd—whom I mostly called "*T*" in those days—had some talent and skill about Dad and was able to charm, cajole, persuade, and argue his way through many more conflicts with our father than I could even dream of. Of course, T's tactics didn't always work, but I so admired his ability to keep his cool, talk things through, and get somewhere in disagreement with our father. Todd was unfazed when Dad went off, sending Tate II through the roof! I did not have such talent or skill. I just capitulated to all his demands. And, whether it was me, T, or our Mom he was dealing with, Dad had this piercing, laser-beam stare. It melted me and made me feel broken. I'd just fall apart.

In his defense, I guess Dad had gotten used to being in power and didn't understand how not to bring it home. He had been to Stanford as an undergrad and for law school. He knew all the right people and, as I found out later, had become a seriously dangerous player in LA's version of the Old Boys Club. Nor was this only an LA thing, but statewide, regional, and national. (Sometimes my theme lyrics for Dad were *I'm bad, I'm nationwide,* by ZZ Top) Yes, he was cruel as a father, but this cold cruelty was part of what made him a powerful and highly respected lawyer. It's creepy, but it's true.

And so, powerless in my father's realm, I was an engaged kid in school. Not only did I excel as a student and participate in extracurricular activities, but I also embraced that stuff. There was a uniform at school and a uniform for life away from school, too. It was called *Preppy*—a Polo or Izod shirt, Levi 501s or khakis, and either the right kind of Top-Siders or tennis shoes. By the time I was in high school, I had successfully refined my social skills and manners to the degree that my parents and their friends accepted me as befitting the description of a fine young man.

I enjoyed playing tennis and showed aptitude. Once I showed some talent, my parents insisted I become a competitive player, so I had a coach and regular lessons. As previously discussed, I was brought up to play to win, and not just on the court. Life was a game to be won, and the tennis court at the country club, along with the immediately peripheral phenomena, was an excellent training ground. So, of course, I didn't even mind that all this was expected of me. I just undertook the brutal schedule of school, playing tennis or having a lesson after school, and through the weekend and studying at night. That was my life, and I embraced it. In retrospect, I apparently didn't have much choice. It was hard, but I handled it. Frankly, as a kid, it gave me a sense of accomplishment and pride.

On the other hand, Todd rejected that kind of charmed life while he was still very young. Dad had to pull some strings to get him into St. Anton's, but he didn't last long: how he hated it there! Parochial Catholic boys' school uniform and short hair are not for Todd.

His uniform was always dirty, and sometimes he lost it. He would hold out as long as possible for a haircut. He always managed to land in the headmaster's office for some infraction or rebellious act. By the winter break, it was apparent that he didn't belong there. I overheard my parents discussing it, my Mom mocking the principal's suggestion that perhaps Todd would be better served at a *public* school, emphasizing that word as if it were an expletive. They fought back. A few more strings got pulled, and the folks tried to come down hard on Todd. He didn't care. He had his bike and knew his way around our part of town, so he was mobile. He was down at the beach all the time and began surfing and hanging out with the wrong crowd. By the end of his freshman year, it turned out that, even though his grades weren't all that bad, he had shown up to class a little more than half the time, probably stoned. Nothing could be done, and he was asked to leave, that is, he got kicked out.

This caused as much unrest at home as I could remember up to that point. It was embarrassing for my parents, and they fought with each other more than ever. It seemed to me like the folks were overreacting, but it was all so much bigger than me. I wanted to defend my brother, who I still thought was the coolest person in the world, but I was just a little kid. So, I hid behind the life built around me and kept going as I had been. Like a machine, I went to school, studied hard, took tennis lessons, and played tennis in my free time at the club.

I was polite, well-mannered, well-groomed, and I did what I was supposed to do. My theme song could have been *You're So Square* by Buddy Holly or the Elvis Presley version when I was at my coolest.

CHAPTER 12

Surf's Up Review

I do not refer to my brother as Tate, but, of course, that was still his name when we were kids. I guess I was ten, and Todd was twelve when the family had our first vacation at Waikiki Beach in Honolulu. We stayed at the Royal Hawaiian. Mom and Dad were focused when it came to vacations. By that, I mean it was important for us to stay at the nicest places on Earth, not only for our comfort and pleasure, but no less for bragging rights at the country club and in their social circle. Remember, we *were* the Joneses.

It was there on the beach at Waikiki that Todd and I truly fell in love with surfing. We were able to take lessons with a real Hawaiian Beach Boy right there at Pops Beach. What a beautiful thing to watch the old-school Hawaiians ride those slow rollers with such exquisite physical grace. The memory of this is burned inside me, and there it is, up on the screen.

Our folks had a general disdain, not for surfing per se, but for the ne'er-do-wells or, as my Dad liked to call them, miscreants who had nothing better to do than bum around the beach all day and smoke pot. Weed notwithstanding, the local surfers back home were the bad element our parents tried so hopelessly to keep us from. In Hawaii, though, surfing was revered, not disregarded by the upper crust. In fact, it was considered *The Sport of Kings* and a healthy art form. The family was also invited to the Outrigger Canoe Club (a prestigious private club founded in 1908). The exclusive invitation was from an old family friend/client of Owen and Owen, who had relocated to Hawaii to become CEO of Dole Foods.

We were sternly admonished that both of us needed to be on our *best behavior.* Surprisingly, Todd complied and seemed to transform immediately into a proper Owen boy because he wanted to surf at the legendary club. It blew me away, and I thought, *Who are you?!* about my older, rebellious, social chameleon brother who could switch from Punk to Preppie in a blink. By that point, he had gotten pretty good on the ukulele. It always amazed me how these massive Hawaiians with massive hands and massive fingers could pull such sweet notes out of a musical instrument, sometimes smaller than their arms.

We'd been taught a few chords by the Beach Boys (no, not the rock group, the Hawaiian dudes), and while I struggled and plunked along, Todd could really play almost right away. One of my earlier lessons in the white v. native interface was that surfing, and the uke were highly pleasing to us both and embraced as de rigueur at the Outrigger.

The most famous Hawaiian of all, Olympian and father of modern surfing Duke Kahanamoku, once said: "Every day of the year where the water is 76, day and night, and the waves roll high, I take my sled, without runners, and coast down the face of the big waves that roll in at Waikiki."

Duke was right, and that's what Todd and I did all day, every day, and it really put the hook in us.

Upon arriving in the afternoon, the trade winds were light offshore, and the waves were rolling perfectly about chest-high out in front of the club. There was a handful of buff, bronzed club members out in the lineup, smiling while bantering with one another. We paddled out with alacrity to join the smiles and were warmly greeted in the warm azure waters. It was an unforgettable experience as the elders were pushing us into waves, and we gradually caught our own: figuring out the fall line and gently sliding our rails into the curvature of the A-framed perfect peelers, overwatched by the broad shoulders of Diamond Head.

Duke got it right: perfect water, winds always just right, tides don't matter, waves for all levels, and plenty of aloha in the water. Crowds didn't matter because you can surf all day, every day. Hard to imagine a better place to get hooked into the Secrets of the Sea than Waikiki.

Famished after surfing, we gorged ourselves on *pupus* (appetizers) and the incredibly delicious buffet and *Ohana* (a Hawaiian term meaning *family*) hospitality—either immediate or extended. To this date, that afternoon/evening remains one of the happiest of my life. I felt alive and loved by everyone, including my parents and brother, and there actually was a strong connection between that day.

For a day, we were *ohana.*

Both the traditional Hawaiian cultural pastimes came home with us, and surfing was already built into the Southern California beach scene we lived in. When we played the ukulele at home, it immediately brought back the Aloha state of mind that Hawaii had exposed us to. When we got back home from that first trip, though the folks frowned upon surfing, they didn't forbid it. We'd both caught the bug, and I've always wondered whether I would have rebelled at that young age if I'd been stopped from doing this beautiful thing. There were rules. I could only go to the *nice* beaches, not the *other kind.* Todd did rebel on that count. He just wouldn't play ball. He'd ride his bike down to the closest beach break where, as our parents tended to put it: the scum meets the surf. About a 15–20-minute ride there, 25–30 minutes partially uphill on the way back.

Todd embraced the culture by wearing puka shells around his neck at all times, much to the chagrin of our parents. No alligator shirts or Top Siders for Todd; his uniform was surfing T-shirts—such as his favorite *Hang Loose* shirt—OP shorts, and flip-flops everywhere he could get away with and grow his hair as long as he could until scissors were forced upon his sun-bleached long locks. He adorned his room with posters of his favorite surfers. Hardly role models by our parents' standards, such as Wayne "Rabbit" Bartholomew, Peter Townend, Michael Peterson, Shaun Tomson, Montgomery "Buttons" Kaluhiokalani, and the Dogtown surfers and skaters from Venice/Santa Monica.

The rebellious teenager surfer might sound like a set of clichés now, but back then—more so in a family like ours—it was no small thing. When Tate III grew his hair out and wore clothing unfit for an Owen boy, my father got surly about his appearance. No matter what Dad said, my brother wouldn't capitulate. Imagine a powerful lawyer making arguments that get him nowhere with his teenage son. Worse yet, since Todd began hanging out with the local surfers, he was buzzed from the prevalent Colombian joints that freely passed around at the beach, in VW buses or Bugs, or whatever surf car was around, pretty much all the time.

Even though I was so young, I could tell this was a recipe for disaster. The folks were at a loss. They just didn't know what to do. The more they tried to lure Todd away from the surf and those characters down there, the more they drove him away from the family. It was as if they were pushing Todd down to the beach. There, he could relate and only be judged on his surfing. The threats of being grounded turned into actually being grounded. He didn't care. He would still get up at the crack of dawn to catch the morning glass, and there wasn't a hell of a lot our folks could do about it.

Todd was a goofy foot (left front forward stance) and developed some style. He was wiry, almost Gumby-like, and seemed to be able to paddle into all kinds of waves. Surfing seemed to be the only thing he could focus on, and that's one of the beautiful things about surfing. It requires focus. Surfing transforms you into a Zen-like state where you can actually "be in the moment." At least there was something for him to focus on! Anyway, without having to try, he developed an identity as a pretty rad surfer. It is certainly not irrelevant to add here, and I would be remiss not to mention that this was when the bikini-clad beach girls came into the picture for him.

What were Tate Jr. and Patricia to do? Their worst nightmare had long been unfolding before their eyes, and now it was in full bloom. Todd had disengaged from their world and had become aloof. They seemed to have some kind of theory about Todd's questionable behavior having a direct correlation with the amount of time he spent at the beach, but they didn't know what to do about it.

When we were younger, Dad would cross-examine us about our day: school, tennis, and perhaps our thoughts on some current event. But, by this point in our lives, Todd had outright contempt for old Tate Jr. and this ritual. It had turned into a battle of Dad scolding Todd and Todd sneering and almost snarling in an effort not to respond. He knew what would happen if he said anything to cross our father. We both knew.

As one might expect, this family rift caused incredible pain and anguish. I have loved and looked up to my brother since I was born. But this situation was more than I could handle. How dare I take Todd's side, yet I couldn't take my parents' side, either. I was overwhelmed with internal conflict about this for a long time. I struggled just trying to understand it and probably never really did. And, if I ever did, I most likely did all I could to suppress my true feelings to survive.

None of us seemed to know what to do, though. Mom went along with whatever Dad said. She was so repressed, I never knew how she dealt with all this. She just continued to perform her role in my father's kingdom faithfully. And, yeah, I guess I just did what I could to bury all of it. Those times, it became too much, the whole mess of it bubbling up to the surface, times I wanted to yell back at my father for once, vent the frustration bottled up inside me, tell both of them that Todd was okay and they should just let him be. I found a way to hold it in. I could tell Todd how I felt, but telling my parents was utterly impossible for me; I felt stifled.

I had conscious fantasies of Todd saving us and our escaping. I had dreams about it, with visions of us together at the beach in LA and Hawaii. Sometimes they were calm, sweet, and lovely, and sometimes they turned to nightmares. In these *disaster dreams,* things are going wrong with strangers or our parents showing up or people at the clubs at both places, some of whom did and others who didn't exist in reality. I can't say I entirely understand it, even now. I remember this one part of me, for whatever reason—perhaps simply the fear of my father—doing what I had to do to stay within the lines. In retrospect, I would characterize it as an autopilot based on an insane premise, as some mad scientist wrote the program. Indeed, the last image on the screen zoomed out from one of my dreams gone wrong to reveal a man in a lab coat watching over the entire scene, clipboard in hand, observing and taking notes.

The screen suddenly goes white, and the light comes up, yet there is no courtroom below. The Buddha and I are sitting in that same space, now afloat in the area. A distinct sense of shame makes me hesitate before looking up and over at the Buddha. When I do, he is not smiling, nor does he frown. He is simply with me, beaming love and compassion. There appears to be some kind of light show radiating out of him, rainbows and laser beams flying all around, but this is not the lesson. It begins to rain. It is a rain of love and compassion. I was so bathed in his energy of forgiveness that it enveloped my heart and allowed me to forgive all and come home to life again. His lips do not move, yet I heard his warm voice say: "It is done. So be it."

CHAPTER 13

Back in the Body

I woke up in a state where my body felt so heavy and listless that I wondered if I had a stroke or was in a coma, but I didn't feel that bad—I just couldn't move. Then I realized I could move, but needed some time to take it all in. So, I laid there for around fifteen minutes, processing God knows what. Or maybe Buddha knows what, I mused. I knew I'd been through something surreal. I remembered a weird courtroom where I was on trial, my family history, a Buddhist teacher, waves of love and compassion, and forgiveness. It is done. So be it. So be what? I realized there were recurring aspects to the dream, yet I felt most of it already slipping away like ocean waves receding from the beach.

I showered as soon as I could get up and calculated how my range of thought and feeling had expanded and intensified since my personal disaster. I felt lighter and heavier. I was more tired when tired and more energized when full of energy. I was happier than usual when happy and, wow, yes, far more deeply depressed when depressed. Mentally sharper at times, a complete dullard at others. I felt everything so intensely at one extreme or another. I wondered whether my brain was being more efficient, as if I'd received an upgrade of sorts, or if this was just me getting crazier and crazier.

My entire caseload had been reassigned, but some details still required my attention. My secretary Sherry would come to the house with things requiring my signature and, perhaps, though far less likely, my consideration, which was the correct play anyway since I was usually too fried to bring much focus to any matter. I remember giving up on whatever she had to say almost right away, signing whatever she put in front of me, and telling her to do whatever she thought best.

My parents did not come over, not once. Sure, I could've gone to their house. I mean, I suppose they would have let me in to talk things over, but I couldn't make it over there! I could barely exit my front door! They didn't even call to check up on me. I called my Mom soon after it happened, but she just unsympathetically echoed Dad's disappointment. Ah, that sound of disappointment in my mother's voice cut me profoundly to the core. And then she came up with a lame excuse to get off the phone. I didn't call again.

Todd came through. He'd somehow heard about what happened and just showed up one day without an inkling of resentment about the past. He started coming over every day and did his best to cheer me up. He was even able to make me feel somewhat sane for a while, which always helped calm me down.

Horrified by my self-destructive diet, Todd and Sherry brought healthy food with them, knowing it would have to be food that required little to no prep. I continued with my Top Ramen, SpaghettiOs, and takeout, but they mainly brought me such beautiful fruits that, depressed and wacky as I was, it was simply irresistible. Mangoes, papayas, apples, pears, oranges, berries of all kinds, and organic. In retrospect, I think eating those fruits regularly helped me fight through the depression.

A third person was coming over, too: my long-time housekeeper, Lorena. Over the years, I'd never had a proper conversation with her. Her only significance was to clean my place, so besides pointing and our brief conversations in Spanglish, I overlooked the fact that she was even a human being, let alone a sweet, honest, hardworking woman. I certainly saw things differently because of where I was at; I realized I'd always taken her for granted. Usually, I'd just tell her what I needed, and she did it, rarely looking me in the eye.

At this point, though, we started talking and looked at each other when we did. I was lounging around the house most of the day, and I welcomed any human contact. When I tried to apologize for all the years of ignoring her, she shrugged it off, smiled as if to appreciate the gesture, and said in broken English: "I am used to it. You, not the only one."

Lorena had such kind, caring eyes, which I'd never noticed before. She understood I was in trouble, and with true unconditional empathy, she did what she could to comfort me and, believe it or not, seemed to have actual feelings for me. She cared even though I had, regrettably, always treated her as a servant. Her poor English embarrassed her, but I loved it. We actually helped one another: I corrected her English while she taught me more Spanish. And I would never have known that she had this tremendous compassion and understanding of life if not for this breakdown of mine.

Nor did she ever even complain about the God-awful mess she invariably walked into. I suppose it annoyed her, but she never allowed me to think so. She'd come in, greet me, see if I needed anything done right away or wanted to talk for a little while, then get down to pick up after me. Pizza boxes, takeout containers, soda cans, plates, glasses, and whatever else was lying around. It probably didn't smell that good, either. I just couldn't deal with anything. I was too busy feeling sorry for myself, ruminating about the wrong turn my life had taken, and just trying to keep my head above the despair and misery. She had been coming to work for me once a week, but I asked, and she agreed to come twice. I liked the company, and she desperately needed the money, as she was just making ends meet. For the first time in my life, I cared about someone *lesser than myself.* I felt sorry for her, wanted to help her out, and we both enjoyed the company.

By then, Todd had developed something like a spiritual presence. I would describe him as seriously mild. Many years before, rehab finally took him, and then Alcoholics Anonymous (AA), along with a good talk therapist, brought him a very long way. He traded his old habits for meditation, eastern mystical thought, and what are referred to as new-age books. I remember mocking him about the self-help stuff when he started to get into it, but he got a lot out of it.

The recurring themes in these books generally involve approaches to improving one's life, mainly through adjusting one's perspective toward acceptance and developing a deep sense of gratitude. I'd been born and bred to be a ruthless, ambitious lawyer! What the hell was I supposed to do with any of that?! I took none of it seriously, and it widened the gap between us all those years ago. I was certainly happy for him that he could get sober and put some kind of life together, which he did magnificently. There didn't seem to be much of a place in it. He'd been in and out of all kinds of trouble up to that point. Along with the programs, self-help, etc., it was all too earnest and sweet for me.

Once he found out what had happened to me, Todd came over every day or at night to support me. He'd just sit and listen to me vent about the unfairness of the world. He'd nod with that goofy grin and try to get me to see that I needed to accept what had happened as a gift with which I could raise my level of consciousness and move on from there. I needed to come to terms with the fact that the world wouldn't change for me. I would have to change. Todd never raised his voice, even when I did. He was bringing me good company, good cheer, good food, and good books, the latter of which I never read until much later. He didn't give up on me, though—he kept showing up. And, of course, he was right. My life was bound to begin anew after this experience with Bianca. It was up to me how.

It was highly relevant to Todd that I had stopped surfing. I didn't play tennis much anymore, either. Sure, if there were some reasons to show up at some club to play with an important client or potential client, I would do so, but I'd misplaced my love for both these sports, and the world of tennis is so different from that of surfing, anyway. After we'd talked for a while and he'd gained my confidence, which only took a few days (I didn't really trust him at first), Todd and I began to go surfing together. He wouldn't take no for an answer, and there were no two ways about it. After getting on board again, I was astounded that I could have left this most beautiful thing behind. I don't even remember how it happened, aside from the fact that, at some point, I decided I simply didn't have the time anymore. He insisted we surf together, which was a key aspect of my road back to life.

During the 1990s, the Gotcha surf wear company had a campaign that proclaimed: IF YOU DON'T SURF, DON'T START. IF YOU SURF, DON'T STOP. And they were right. This was my credo.

One good result of my support was that I slept a little better. There really is something to this idea of how simplifying your life can relieve anxiety, though I don't know if I would have made much progress without Todd. I often wonder what would have happened to me if he hadn't shown up on my doorstep. Getting in the ocean every day helped, too.

As time went by, I had the impression that I was shedding layer after layer of all that had been keeping me from my true self. I wondered if, maybe, by osmosis, the Buddha experiences were affecting my daily life. It isn't much fun to face the fact that you were a horrible person who did awful things and may still be, but it felt wonderful to witness these aspects of that person leaving me bit by bit. The vanity, the obsession with wealth and power, and the idea that I am better than others and that my money, holdings, position, education, and background, even my car and my watch, are signs of my superiority, all helped perpetuate the idea that women are to be bought.

And, worst of all, that love is a scam. These ideas were not only leaving me, but I was becoming aware they were barriers to the real me, and it had started to make me happy in a whole new way to see a life without them. The phenomenon opened my heart. That flesh and blood muscle was glowing from the inside and sending out waves of pink light to the Universe. As I got into bed one night, feeling as good as I had in a long time, I felt the following phrase rise from my heart and out of my mouth sincerely: "I want to learn a better way to live my life."

CHAPTER 14

The Three Priceless Techniques

Somewhere between being awake and asleep, I heard a somehow familiar voice. Perhaps I was dreaming, maybe not, but it seemed like I had just settled into bed for a few moments before I heard: “Dale, the life you wish for is possible, and you can have it.” The Buddha’s voice continued: “The world of Maya that you have been living in is just an illusion in your mind.” The Buddha was sitting cross-legged, hovering in the air in the middle of the room. His radiance, as before, showered me with euphoria. Clearly, there was more for me to learn if I was going to stop the misery that I, with my own mind and emotions, was creating for myself and those around me.

The ever-perceptive Buddha smiled and said: “Now, I will teach you *Three Priceless Techniques* that will transform your illusion and, thus, you’re suffering. Before I teach you the *First Priceless Technique*, what do you see when you look at yourself in the mirror?” Suddenly, I was standing before a full-length mirror. While I looked in the mirror, I saw a man who was tired, losing his hair, his youth long gone, with bags under his eyes and wrinkles on his forehead. I summed up my existence by answering the Buddha with: “I see a middle-aged lawyer.” Then, just as suddenly, I was back in bed.

I didn't notice any change in his expression as he spoke. However, the compassion pouring out of him was palpable: "My dear, *The First Priceless Technique* is to remember that you are a Buddha and that you have a Buddha Nature."

"I am a Buddha… What does it mean?"

The Buddha paused for a moment and then said with great clarity: "It means you are awake! It means you see past the Maya, living outside this world of physical illusion. A Buddha ceases experiencing the anguish, misery, and suffering that you have been living through in your life. A Buddha is filled with *tranquil abiding*, deep peace, empathy, and compassion."

He went on: "Unfortunately, Dale, you are blocking your true *Buddha Nature.* As you continue to identify yourself with the world of illusion, that world will continue to engulf you, and all your thoughts and emotions will go along with it. As many people like to say these days, you must lighten up, yes?"

He giggled before continuing: "Enlightenment simply means to lighten one's state of mind. All that heaviness, all those negative emotions, and thoughts all seem so important until you realize they are part of an illusory world. And so, the first step is to remember that you are a Buddha."

I remember thinking that taking this idea was like trying to drink from a fire hose. For a moment, it occurred to me that I wouldn't be able to understand these teachings, much less deploy them. I mean, what the hell is tranquil abiding? If he could read my mind or my expression, there was not an inkling of impatience with my moment of doubt. That impervious compassion of his rolled over me and brought a tear to my eye. My thought was: "I want this," and I pulled back into the zone.

"How do I remember?" I queried.

"It's really quite simple," answered the Buddha. "Close your eyes, set your tongue on the roof of your mouth, and imagine that you are a Golden Buddha. Right there, in your bed, imagine you are a Golden

Buddha, and fill yourself entirely, from head to toe, with pure, bright, and glowing golden light. Once you have accomplished this, imagine a rainbow emanating in concentric circles all around you. Continue to imagine the concentric circles of that rainbow emanating outward to infinity, all the while continuing to see yourself as a Golden Buddha."

It took some time, and I wasn't quite sure about the Buddha part, but very soon after, I was able to see myself as a being imbued with golden light; I also felt my chest getting warmer and warmer and a sense of joy rising with the heat. With each passing moment, along with the joy, there was also a kind of peace I don't believe I had ever experienced before, which grew deeper and deeper. Whatever tension I had been holding in my shoulders released somehow, and I felt my upper thorax, neck, and head spread out wide on the bed. My breathing became deeper and slower, and my face felt like it was glowing. At a certain point, I could open up and let the rainbow flow outward as prescribed. Yes. Then, with the peace and joy flowing so beautifully through and through, I found myself experiencing two other states of being that I was not at all used to—humility and gratitude—at what seemed like extraordinarily profound levels. I let it be for a while until I managed to say to the Buddha: "I'm free."

He didn't respond for a while. Everything was lovely, and I thought it very generous of him to let me be. After that kind pause, he spoke again: "Dale, the intended result of this *First Priceless Technique* is to bring you back to your true nature, your *Buddha Nature*. Before we get to the *Second Priceless Technique*, I would like to offer you an advanced aspect of the First that you may use at your pleasure."

"Please visualize a Golden Buddha descending from the heavens, or more specifically, the aspect of the heavens the Buddhists call Tushita, where Bodhisattvas abide before incarnating on Earth. Visualize a Golden Buddha coming down and in through the top of your head. Do it now."

The Buddha waited until I had done so, then continued: "As you bring the Golden Buddha in through the top of your head and into your body, merge with the Buddha so that the two of you become one. I shall wait until you can tell me that you have done so."

He paused again, this time until I could confirm the conscious act: "Good. Now that you have accomplished this: visualize your rainbow in concentric circles of color and light spiraling out in all ten directions. It may seem simple, and perhaps it is, but it is definitely profound as well. Remember this in the future: it is imperative to the Technique's success as you practice merging with the Buddha at the beginning. It will, at once, bring you the tranquility and empowering energy that will help you cultivate your Buddhahood. This state will then allow you to begin to bring about the intended result of the vision of the rainbow emerging from your heart center, which is to transform the surrounding environment into one of peace, tranquility, love, and compassion."

Another sagacious pause. It had become quite clear that the Buddha's repertoire included impeccable timing. As I lay there in my bed, utterly at peace, filled with light, finding a home in my very own heart, I suddenly had a thought that struck me as hilarious. The thought was simple: I'm a lawyer. The utter absurdity that I would limit myself to a vision of myself as something such as that, when all the multiverses were mine, for asking if I would just present with enough humility to share it. Well, I laughed and couldn't stop. I became absolutely hysterical, tears of release streaming out that became part of the rainbow. Such joy, such joy! That I had been identifying myself as a lawyer for so long that I somehow chose to limit myself to that was *mind-bendingly* funny. Tip-of-the-iceberg-type stuff vis-à-vis my true existence, and within a split second in the dream, I had a massive vision about the gap between who we think we are and who we are meant to be.

After I'd been writhing with it like that for a while, the Buddha asked: "What is it, little brother? We can always use a good joke." So, I told him, though it took a few attempts because by the time I thought to say it, it was just too funny to get it out before laughing again. Finally, I managed to tell him: "I'm a lawyer."

He responded: "Oh, yes, I see," and began laughing with me. Ah, the beauty of this exquisite being's laughter! It filled the room with love, and it appeared that light forms flashed out of him like lightning, rainbows, and laser beams. Higher and higher it rose, both of us, until we were roaring with it, and I had another vision of our laughter, through him, rising higher and higher until the Bodhisattvas in the Tushita could hear it and laughed with us as if the joy and release were something that could be shared with these grand beings and the whole of the planet and then the whole of the universe. We all laughed until we could laugh no more and then we were at peace and so very clear and happy.

CHAPTER 15

Priceless Techniques Two and Three

We finally simmered down and spent quite a long stretch in that deep golden peace. At some point, the Buddha spoke again: "It is now time for you to learn *Priceless Technique Number Two,* Dale. Let us begin. When you look at your world, what do you see?" Piecing together my life review, I thought of all the conflict at home and at school during my childhood, and conflict once I'd gone out into the world on my own, and so very much conflict in the professional world as an adult. I thought of all the craziness with Bianca and a few other romances gone wrong. I said, "My world is full of conflict! It's a dark place."

He paused, then began: "Very good, my dear. The world, as you are currently seeing it, from the ego's perspective, is very much about conflict, which leads to sadness and suffering. While there are times of happiness, these times are fleeting, and suffering is inevitable. Buddhists call this world of suffering *Samsara*—the cycle of death and rebirth to which life in the material world is bound. As you learn to see the world through your Buddha Nature, you will move past the world of form and illusion that is plaguing you and others."

Buddha continued: "Since you are now in the process of remembering that you are a Buddha, you must also remember that the location you are in, wherever you presume to be, is a *Buddha Field.* The energy that radiates from your Buddha presence inherently helps transform the surrounding environment into a *Buddha Field,*" he clarified.

Priceless Technique Number Two is seeing the environment around you and the world in general as a *Buddha Field.* You must learn to look past the illusion and see the environment for what it is: Pure Radiant Light!" as he said this, his own light radiated purely.

"Relative to the way that you saw yourself merely as an attorney, from that limited perspective, one can only see a world of conflict and darkness. As a Buddha in a *Buddha Field*, you can help transform it." I looked around my bedroom and tried to imagine the world around me transforming into a *Buddha Field.* The Buddha, still glowing in gold, helped me begin as the golden light shining through him expanded until my darkroom was finally bright with gold and blue and white light. If this was all a dream, it was a good one, as I was also very wide awake and very much at peace and would take these dreams every day to my everyday reality. It dawned on me that peace had levels and that I was beginning to understand it more deeply. One aspect of peace showed itself. I noticed that my inner chatter had stopped, and I was bathed in silence. The light I was seeing was filled with waves of energy. This level of consciousness enabled me to feel deeper and deeper levels of peace, stillness, and love.

The Buddha knew: "Very good, Dale. You are learning quickly, but you must remember to keep at it. Your disciplined practice will create your freedom from suffering." My mind interrupted his flowing stream of consciousness, and I mentally noted this powerful communication.

The Buddha momentarily paused, as he could probably hear my interjecting thoughts, then resumed: "As you continue to practice, it will become even easier to imagine that you are a Buddha and that all that is around you is a *Buddha Field.* Over time, with practice and compassion, you will transform into this state of being. So Be It. Are you ready for *Priceless Technique Number Three?*"

I was feeling so high and exalted, rapt in a clear sailing kinda mode, that I exuberantly blurted out: "YES!"

The Buddha continued: "Once again, we are addressing something that, though conceptually quite simple, is not all that easy for most people to accomplish. Now, imagine seeing someone you love."

I immediately thought of my brother.

"Now, Dale, think of someone you don't like very much. Indeed, think of someone you definitely loathe." I immediately pictured Bianca, in full costume, as a witch. But not that hot witch I had dreamt of before. This was pure wicked witch-of-the-west-type stuff—the full black costume, pointy hat, green face, and horrible cackle that are right down to the "Yes, my pretty."

"What is the difference in the way you perceive these people?" I had never really thought about it like that. The way I saw people. The Buddha was not asking about the good and the bad of people. He was asking about the nature of my perception. It just seemed normal to judge others off the top of my head. I thought for a moment and replied: "I guess, to be fair, with Todd, I'm focused on his good qualities. When it comes to Bianca, though, the negatives seem unavoidable."

The Buddha started anew, "As we've discussed, and you seem somewhat comfortable with it now, the world you have been living in is an illusory dream built on your preconceptions. What is considered the physical world is not the true ground of reality. The true ground of reality, the real world, as they say, is a world of energy. In our forays into your remembrance of your *Buddhahood* and your visions of the *Buddha Fields*, you have already experienced this."

Buddha paused for that to sink in, then: "When you find yourself angry or very upset with family members or those in your work environment, such thoughts and emotions emanate from your non-Buddha nature. The negative preconceptions you hold toward these people project negative energies at them to make matters worse. These negative energies affect their internal organs and their energy fields and injure their Buddha Nature. Along with this damage to them, there is also a rebound effect; that is to say, it damages you, as well."

Another pause, for Buddha, was patient and then: "Since you are in the process of remembering that you are a Buddha, you are obliged to practice the Buddhist principle of Ahimsa, which means noninjury. By applying this principle, you are not to hurt anyone physically, nor are you to hurt anyone with your mind, thoughts, or speech."

Buddha took a longer pause for this to take root. I don't believe I had ever considered that one could really harm another person with thought.

"Each person, whether you choose to like them or not, is just like you in the sense that he or she is just another person on their way to remembering their Buddha Nature. Some are farther down the path than others. Many have barely started. And so, *Priceless Technique Number Three* is to remember that all others are Buddhas on the path, too, and that you must see them as such. Let's try an experiment. Imagine yourself at the office. Let's use your father since he is both your boss and your family. It is the end of the year, and the two of you are sitting in his office. He compliments you on how well you've been doing and what a great year you've had, and he is very proud of you. Then he concludes by telling you that you needed to do much better the next year because there is an attorney at the firm, a contemporary of yours, who had had just as good a year as you did. Perhaps he was simply trying to motivate you, but because of how you see him and how he acts, it feels more like a threat," he shared with startling omnipotence.

At first, I remember it being disconcerting that the Buddha had grabbed onto something that happened, especially since there is so much that I am ashamed of in my life and would prefer not to feel so exposed. Yet, one look over at him, seeing him beaming at me with such impeccable compassion, was all I needed to go on with the experiment.

"Now imagine yourself in that situation becoming, as you have done before PT1, a Buddha of pure golden light with the rainbow beaming out from your Buddha self into the room, transforming it into a *Buddha Field.* Then imagine your father turning into a Buddha of pure golden light by applying *Priceless Technique Number Three.*"

I wasn't sure what the Buddhist equivalent of church bells going off was, but I could swear I heard something to that effect when he finished with this statement.

It didn't seem very likely that I would be able to see my father as a Golden Buddha, but I followed the steps of the *Technique*, and much to my amazement, the scenario was magically altered. It was instantly clear that my father was simply passing on some information that he thought would be of use to me. His compliments were sincere, and the remarks that had to do with the up-and-coming lawyer were somehow passed along warmly instead of with his usual caustic effect. I'd always remembered that meeting with resentment, and now I was able to say something to myself that I hadn't in a very long time: "Wow, my father really loves me." I couldn't remember ever having any insight into the way my father thought, except as the killer attorney I perceived him to be, and now this… what… healing? It was absolutely unbelievable.

This *Priceless Technique* was the crown jewel of the 3PTs!

I asked: "How many people know about these Three Priceless Techniques?" The Buddha replied with, "Clearly not enough." I mentally cajoled him as I felt there was a hint of sarcasm in the Buddha's reply or possibly a lament on his part, as there was a lot of work for him to do in the years ahead. Maybe, on some level, since I was the Buddha and the Buddha was me, it was me who realized how much work lay ahead of me!

I blurted out somewhat excitedly but also reluctantly, not wanting to know the answer: "Well, how many would be enough?" Buddha said, "Excellent question, my dear! We believe that if seven million or more would apply The Three Priceless Techniques simultaneously, it could create a wave of energy, literally a tsunami of positive energy that, if done correctly, would transform the physical world into a *Buddha Field...* forever. Relatively speaking, of course. In the future, you will help with this, Dale; however, we have come very far tonight, and it is time for you to rest and process all that you have learned and experienced."

With that, the Buddha vanished before my eyes, and I was alone in my bed in my dark room, as if nothing had happened. Just as suddenly, I realized how completely exhausted I was and trailed off to sleep.

The Morning After

It was well into the afternoon when I woke up groggy and was surprised by Todd lounging on the couch in my bedroom. "Sup, bro? Have something to eat, and let's grab some waves. How long have you been sitting there?" he said.

"I dunno, ten minutes," I yawned.

"You still snore. And you were babbling about some Three Priceless Techniques?"

"Give me something to write with."

Todd grabbed a pen and pad off the end table by the couch and walked them over to me: "What?"

Slightly impatient, I responded: "Just wait a sec," and scribbled out the framework of all three of the techniques. I wasn't really remembering. It was just coming through me.

Framework for The Three Priceless Techniques:

1. Remember that you are a Buddha and have a Buddha Nature.
2. See the environment around you and the world in general as a *Buddha Field.*
3. See that others are Buddhas on the path, too, and envision them as such.

I handed the pad back to Todd. He read it and looked at me in dead earnest: "Wow, that is deep! How'd you come up with *that*?"

"I learned it in a dream that was 'realer' than our speaking now."

That seemed to captivate Todd. The tone of my voice was different, and my words carried a purposefulness that wasn't there before. We both could hear the change. Simultaneously, I could sense he was also feeling something different from me. Possibly, a new field of energy emitting from me.

I was still processing my dream experience and wasn't ready to share it fully. So, I changed the subject to fun: *let's hit some waves!* Todd agreed, and we were off to our playground—the beach. The sun was out, the sky was blue, the sand was warm, and the water was beautiful and extra clear. For a split second, I remembered Priceless Technique Number Two and thought: "Yeah, this is a *Buddha Field*!"

We spent some time looking at the ocean, slowly waxing our boards, and I felt very much at ease. We paddled out together. The water was just fine; no wetsuits were required. The afternoon sun was glistening over a true-blue sea in a cloudless sky. The waves were big that day, just about head high, and not all that well-formed. The wind was light and side shore. It was about 5 p.m. by the time we made our way into the lineup.

Todd greeted friends. Some of the older guys recognized me as Todd's brother, and we said, "Hey." Todd jumped right in, shredding away, while I sat outside of the pack and watched the waves roll in and by for a while. Finally, I thought I'd grab one, so I paddled for it, felt the energy of the wave behind me, realized I wasn't in the right spot, and didn't pull back or get to my feet before the whitewater engulfed me. The energy spits me forward far enough for the wave to break on my back. It was such a bonehead, amateur maneuver that I was laughing at myself when I came up for air, only to turn around to see another wave breaking right in my face. I actually heard the water slap me in the face! My board and I tumbled along, and I guess I was lucky not to get too hurt, but it seemed so much funnier than dangerous that by the time I had tumbled almost all the way in and was able to get on my feet, I was caught between laughing at myself and clearing out the cobwebs. I'd shaken it off by the time Todd paddled up to me to make sure I was okay.

"What the hell are you smiling at? Although it *was* entertaining. You okay?"

"I'm a doofus!"

"You're a Buddha! Who forgot how to surf!"

"Yup."

We laughed and paddled outside the break together again. I caught a few little inside waves over the next hour or so. I couldn't wipe that smile off my face. It also occurred to me that it was a good thing to wipe out like that and be reminded of the ocean's power. This was the first practical lesson in my spiritual path—not to take myself too seriously.

"*The final illusion is power, while laughter is the final truth.*"

—Peter Berger

There was a strange and beautiful moment after my best and last ride of the day. I rode it all the way to the beach, climbing and dropping a shoulder-high-plus peeler. Low clouds had pushed down the coast and were hovering close by as the sun was getting ready to do its sunset show. It can get really sweet when there are little cloud forms clinging to the coast after the sun goes down. I was alone just after finishing that last best ride and decided to head in for the day when I saw something taking shape amidst the clouds. Todd was on the next wave and came to the beach right behind me. For a moment, this Buddha-like figure was seated, beatific, at peace. His expression did not change, yet there seemed to be a wink and a nod of encouragement anyway. The beauty of it choked me and brought a tear to my eye. Then, just as quickly as the vision had come together, it disassembled and was just a group of cloud forms again. I paddled in.

Todd and I sat on the beach for a while after the sunset, and I was in fine shape. The sun was down, the dusk holding on, and a full moon had already shown its face to the southwest. I told him about my vision of the Buddha and was able to talk to him about the dream or experience or whatever it was from the night before. Again, as I think back on his responses, I realize how blessed his presence was through all this. He didn't tell me I was going crazy, nor did he say that now everything was fine and there was nothing further to be done. I remember what he said very well: "The thing about stuff like this is, you have to practice. One does not just get fixed for good, and that's all there is to it. You have to do it every day and, really, build the discipline to sustain that kind of consciousness as close to 24/7 as possible."

We got hungry and decided to go to an old favorite of both of ours, a little place called La Alma Real (The Real Soul, this time, it had some true meaning). Many moons and waves had passed since we'd been there together. A beautiful little casita-style building on the coast highway, there for decades, that we'd been going to since we were little kids with our parents. As you know, I didn't get out very much at all at the time, and this authentic, warm, old-school, family-run Mexican joint charmed me right down to my toes that night. I drank plenty of beer as I scarfed down a delicious shrimp burrito. Todd didn't drink beer, but equally enjoyed his veggie tacos—and it felt like a celebration of sorts. Carlos, who was the current elder now (about our age), whose folks had passed, welcomed us like old amigos.

We finished our dinner, and I ordered another beer. Being in a place we had been to as small children a thousand times after, we had a moment where we looked into each other's eyes, and everything stopped. Time itself seemed to unwind, and we were silent for a while. We were, at once, those little kids as well as the middle-aged men sitting there then. Suddenly, all there was between us was love. How can I impart to you the beauty of a moment like that, dear reader? I can only encourage you to go find the love between you and your brothers and sisters, whether they are your actual siblings or not, and stay there for as long as you can manage it.

Sure, you are free to keep fighting and finding reasons not to be at peace with those around you. Or choose love.

CHAPTER 16

Life Is a Trip

The time had come. I had the tools and had pulled through the most devastating aspects of the crisis, and it was time for me to consider what the rest of my life was going to be about.

The next day, Todd and I sat down with a pad and pen to try to devise a plan of action. We'd broken it down to the immediate problems at hand and ideas about some ultimate goals for my life. As children, we would occasionally go sailing with Poppa on the fine old wooden ketch he'd bought himself when he semi-retired. Oddly enough, like a tried-and-true defense attorney, he renamed her *Demurrer: An objection that an opponent's point is irrelevant or invalid while granting the factual basis of the point.*

When Todd started getting into trouble when we were kids, he'd talk about going down to Marina Del Rey, swiping Dad's boat, and sailing away to Hawaii or another exotic surf location down in the vast, wave-rich coast south of us. Now, that childhood fantasy could finally come to fruition, with nowhere to go and all day to get there.

The *Demurrer* was lonely and bouncing around expensively, unused and forgotten at a slip in the Marina. She was a 1986 42-foot Catalina. Now, Dad owned it, but no one ever used it, though I suppose trysts of some form or another had taken place on or in her over the years. A crew maintained it, and we'd occasionally visit it or hop on board to cruise around the Marina. It hadn't actually been properly sailed for several years. When Poppa bought it new, it was the state of the art.

At any rate, adolescent fantasy or not, sailing to Hawaii certainly made a list. We also listed a trip down the west coast of Mexico and Central America. There are a lot of fantastic breaks along the way, only accessible by boat, and though he'd been to specific places like that one at a time over the years, Todd had never gotten around to making that one long, beautiful surf trip. It didn't sound bad. These thoughts, of course, did not make it onto the Immediate Problems side of the page.

(Lots of travel and adventure theme songs here: *Over the Hills and Far Away* by Led Zeppelin or maybe *Kashmir. Kathmandu* by Bob Seger, but I kinda liked *The Wanderer* by Dion: "*Oh well I roam from town to town/I go through life without a care/'Til I'm as happy as a clown/With my two fists of iron and I'm going nowhere.*"[4])

We considered many options that were ultimately set aside. Once we'd boiled it all down, the first thing was to face the situation at Owen & Owen as best I could and let the chips or guillotine—fall. We both knew—though I was doing far better than I had been three weeks before that moment in time—it would be foolish to pretend that I had gotten it all together and was good to go as Dale Owen of Owen & Owen. Fair to say, I had crawled from the wreckage and was ready to try at least to face the matters at hand.

After Todd left, I sat down at my computer and typed up the plan of action we'd come up with. In the morning, on a Tuesday, I intended to show up at the office at 10 a.m. As a courtesy, and for my own sake, I sent a blanket email addressed to my father but cc'ing everyone else at the firm, informing them that I would be coming in. The email read:

---

[4] "Wanderer," Dion & Ernie Maresca, (Runaround Sue), 1961. This line is excerpted from the song; all rights to the original composition and recording are reserved by the artists and distributors.

> Dear Dad et al.,
>
> I will be there in the morning at 10 a.m. and very happy to answer any and all queries about the Biotrimus matter and/or anything else anyone wants or needs to have my address. I look forward to helping defend the firm in any way I can and am very sorry and, indeed, quite ashamed of the exposure I've opened us up to. You and the partners can consider me completely at your disposal as we work through this unfortunate matter, and I look forward to doing whatever I can to help, as well as, if plausible, the support of the firm since I have so foolishly compromised myself, and made such a mess of the situation, and need all the help I can get.
>
> I apologize, I apologize, I apologize.
>
> Respectfully,
>
> Dale

I didn't sleep all that well—half expecting and hoping for a Buddha visit, but I did get a few hours, and it almost felt like enough. In the morning, I showered, shaved, and realized I needed a haircut. I also realized that my countenance had changed. This was not the same guy in the mirror a few weeks before. I put on one of my best Hugo Boss suits, a Hermes tie, and a lucky old pair of Gucci's. I realized that I hadn't worn a suit for some time. I was in a suit almost every day previously, except weekends and *Casual Fridays,* in which I'd wear a nice button-down or polo shirt when it was hot, slacks, and closed-toed shoes. When I was looking at myself in the mirror, I brought down the

Golden Buddha and improvised with imaging, putting on my *Buddha Suit!* With the stress upcoming, my experience certainly was not as monumental as donning it for the first time in my Buddha Dream, but it didn't move the needle in the right direction!

I got in the car. It was a different trip to the office. I didn't listen to the radio or any music. I drove calmly, in silence, and with no rush, observing people and things in a way I hadn't before, even though I'd made this drive a hundred times, probably thousands of times. Even at 9 a.m., the roads of LA were still packed. Flashing into my head was Priceless Technique Number Two. Ah, I reminded myself to see my surroundings as a *Buddha Field.* I imagined the cars as metallic lotus flowers transporting their serene Buddha passengers. I chuckled at this impromptu visualization and hoped the Buddha would be proud of my improvisation.

I was only cut off three times in my commute, given the finger only once, and nearly hit a car unexpectedly braking in front of me, and still, despite these and a whole host of other minor issues, my drive was surprisingly serene. This technique worked! And, of all days, I needed a little extra help—this was it.

I pulled into my spot at 9:50 and walked by the reception desk at 9:55. As I walked through to my office, everyone seemed more nervous than I was, which put me somewhat at ease. It appeared my *Buddha Suit* only frayed minimally as I was holding my serene and sovereign composure. Seeing everyone trying to be cool about seeing me was funny: twisted fake smiles hiding smirks and disapproving frowns. Sherry, who was such a smart cookie, greeted me with a genuinely amused smile as if we shared some secret and nothing was the matter at all. I might as well have been on holiday for a few weeks.

"Good morning, Dale."

"Good morning, Sherry. Please let my father know I'm here."

"Of course."

CHAPTER 17

The Big Meeting

In my honor (dishonor?), the partners had scheduled an emergency boardroom lunch for 1 p.m. When I was informed of this meeting, very unlike a Buddha, it made me anxious, but Sherry kept me busy all morning, distracting me perfectly and effectively using the time. Ingeniously, she had us attend to the low-hanging fruit, which was easy, comforting, and satisfying in that we got through so much of it. As mentioned above, a lot of my caseload had been taken from me, but that didn't include everything. Sherry had me feeling at home at my desk. Sitting there in my comfy chair and feeling almost normal, I mentally addressed my Buddha Suit and attempted a little primping. It made me feel more *Buddha-like!*

I confidently walked into the boardroom at 12:55, but no one was there.

(For a moment, I thought of the scene from *Goodfellas* where two mobsters lead Joe Pesci's character into a room where he is supposed to be made = a *made* man and untouchable. But the room is empty, and Pesci has a brief flash of horror; then they shoot him in the head and leave him for dead. That didn't happen, but it wasn't a nice thought or feeling.)

Someone had arranged for an assortment of sandwiches and an antipasto platter from Bay Cities, a very normal set-up for an in-house meeting, which sat on the service counter with some plates, napkins, silver, and *accouterment*. This was comfort food, and I needed comforting. I took a Godmother, grabbed a Diet Coke from the fridge, and sat where I usually sit. I didn't feel very hungry, so I popped open the can of Diet Coke, took a sip, and braced myself for the excoriation that was sure to come.

I was dressed comfortably and casually, which I had never done before in a *partnership meeting.*

One by one, all the *suits* filed in and blended together, my father last among them. Their slow-motion entry was surreal, almost like they practiced it, or maybe it was my newfound *Buddha Vision,* but things seemed to slow down a little bit. You can't imagine how bizarre it seemed to me that my Dad had a bit of a smirk on his face as if he were somehow amused; that stern effect was nowhere in sight. I flashed on the part of my dream with the Buddha in which I used Priceless Technique Number Three on my Dad, and I could not help but wonder if I'd altered our relationship by altering my perspective about him. I looked at him blankly, not knowing quite what to do or say, and he put up a reassuring hand that said, *Just wait,* and then got on with it once everyone had sat down and taken some food.

Dad scoffed, "We all know why we're here, gentlemen. Greg?" Gregory Horowitz was the subject of the conversation I'd had with my father in both my dream and in reality, just alluded to above. We never clicked, even though we were the same age. Of course, he resented me. How could he not? As far as he was concerned, I was a partner because of my place in the family, while he had worked his way up from his not-even-modest Brooklyn background. He'd been an NYU undergrad and came to the firm after finishing at Boalt Hall in Berkeley and passing the bar on his first try, and I respected all of that. He was an extraordinarily arrogant little shit, but, in his defense, that isn't such a bad quality for a litigator.

Indeed, he was very good in court, and that is no small thing. Yet, I'd felt the bad vibe coming from him from the beginning, and so I returned it in kind. Our interactions had been strictly business throughout our joint tenure at the firm, and we ultimately became each other's competition. We'd had some run-ins over the years, but nothing that couldn't be resolved from above, often in this very room with the people sitting here now. At times like that, I'm sure he considered leaving more than once.

He'd hung in there, made it to partner, and since Owen & Owen is a damn good place to be a partner, we both lived with our mutual disdain.

Just before he started speaking, I made a feeble attempt to apply Priceless Technique Number Three. For a microsecond, I felt even more relieved and viewed Greg compassionately. This peace was quickly replaced with an energetic punch to my solar plexus, and my *Buddha-Vision* waned like the moon eclipsing the light of the sun.

Horowitz began with a sophisticated and educated air about him and still sounded like an educated New Yorker, insincerely but craftily, as he would rather show respect for the family before cutting into me. He would certainly have to be careful not to show too much glee when executing the latter: "We were all very moved by your email of last night, Dale, and we are all in agreement that we will support you in this matter as best we can. We are still deciding whether it would be best to hire outside counsel or deal with it in-house, both in your defense and ours, and we will let you know as soon as we decide. We are also looking into the potential of a countersuit against this Bianca of yours and the Biotrimus entity. Perhaps more than one. We may address Steve, too… ya know, the Senior Associate and ex-D.A., about any criminal aspects in this, we might assert. Would you have any problem with any of that?"

"None."

"Good man. Now, there's no avoiding it, Dale: You have clearly disgraced the firm, all of us in this room, and everyone who works here.

The scuttlebutt is having its effect, not only in dollars and cents but exponentially in the time it has taken all of us to reassure just about every client we have, and I don't mean just yours. Yes, the complaint is public record, so our competitors craftily–probably gleefully—shared it with existing and potential clients. As such, we have lost a few clients over this, but it hasn't been a complete disaster. It's a crisis we have been compelled to handle."

"Yet, this ongoing issue of time... Time, Dale, you know how valuable it is to all of us. And so, though, it is somewhat gratifying to know that you understand how you've compromised us. You are willing to join us in fighting back; it is also so very troubling to note that there was not one person here at the firm in whom you might have confided regarding, frankly, the stupid fucking shit you bought into with these two criminals. It would be bad enough if you had sunk your own ship in this way, and that was all. But we're all in hot water over this now, and it is all your fault."

"We need you to publicly take responsibility for what you've done and assure us that you are with us right down to the end of this, even if it costs you in some way. And it will cost you. But these costs are and will result from what you've done, not what we will ask of you. Indeed, believe it or not, we hope to protect you from any and all harm as much as is humanly possible."

Horowitz looked at me with an expression that was many orders of magnitude less warm than the Buddha's: "Problem?"

"Zero."

Horowitz continued on, laying out the broad strokes of the complaint: where I was exposed and where the firm was exposed. There was very little discussion after that. I was to produce any and all paperwork I had signed and, indeed, had not signed, having to do with this matter, as well as let everyone know if there might be any outstanding documents not in my possession or verbal agreements I might have made. I was to present anything and everything I could in support of my defense and ours, and after an in-house analysis, decisions about going forward would be made, and the next steps would be taken.

When it was all over, my Dad asked perfunctorily: "Anyone have anything else to say?" No one did. "Then excuse us, please. I'd like to talk to my son." These were all exceptional attorneys, usually with something to add, yet they all got up and walked out in silence, heads down.

"Dale," he began, then paused and actually smiled at me, "You fucked up! I don't know how this will all turn out, but this is the time for all of us to get very calm and clear-headed and project an image of confidence, righteous indignation, and certitude. Except for you, that is. I don't know if you can do it, kid, but you need to assume the role of the humble, damaged, innocent defendant as of now. After all, you're the victim here. For any actual wrong you may have done, be it in the eyes of the firm or the bar or the law? Again, humility and, even more importantly, contrition. No bullshit, that's you until further notice."

"There's going to be a vote in my office after I leave you here, and I know how it will go because I engineered it. You will not like it, and you may resent me for it, but I am asking you to trust me long enough to let me explain it all to you after this little charade takes place, and then you can start, or perhaps continue, resenting me and all the rest of it. We've already gone to work on the political side of this, so just keep your shirt on, don't panic, no matter how bad it may look at any given moment, and don't talk to anyone about this outside the firm. You may want to watch who you talk to around her, too."

"For now, I want to leave you with this. You're my son, and I love you. I've always loved you. You're in trouble now. Not insurmountable trouble, but it's real trouble, and I want you to remember that I love you and will do everything I can to take care of you. I guess I was too much of a hardass as a father to you and Tate—uh, Todd—and I apologize for that. It was how I was raised. Boy, did you guys have a good time with Pop? He used to beat the hell outta me. Anyway, the point of focus here is that this is happening simply because you fell in love with a con man. It made you vulnerable. It could happen to just about anyone. Certainly, any man. I thought she was charming, too. Who wouldn't?"

He laughed out loud, "My son, the mark. Oh, well…" and laughed again. I'd never seen him like this. I actually got teary-eyed. It was really kind of beautiful. "Thank you so much, Dad. I'm very touched by this. I wasn't sure that I wasn't gonna be shown the door this morning, family or not, and you are talking to me like this… it's almost worth all the trouble."

"Let's not get carried away. Go home and gather the documents, hard copies, electronics, everything: no judgment calls, son. Bring every last scrap of paper that has to do with this. In fact, print up and organize everything digital you have with Sherry before you go, including every email exchange with Bianca, with John, and with anyone who had anything to do with this business. Yes, personal emails and correspondences are available as well. Figure out an approach to gathering your text exchanges, too."

"I will."

"Good boy."

He took a deep breath, exhaled, and left me there alone. I felt miserable, safe to say, in a state of shock. Yet my father!!! I'd never gotten around to lunch, so I sat there for another fifteen minutes and ate my Godmother. Then I went back to my office with my tail between my legs and told Sherry what we needed to do. We were there till 8 p.m., and I believe we found everything. I drove straight home after that and began to gather what I had as far as hard copies were concerned, which didn't take all that long. By the end of the night, I was shaking my head with regret like Roger Rabbit and continued to do so well into the morning, just beside myself with grief.

Finally, I fell asleep on the couch with my clothes on. The Bliss of Sleep.

CHAPTER 18

Forced Vacation

The implications of what my father said to me led me to believe that I was not going to like the results, but I decided to take his instruction to stay cool and hear him out after all was said and done.

The vote went against me to a large degree, but I was not entirely condemned. I was called to my Dad's office when I got in the next morning, and he explained not only what happened but everything that would happen had to do with all my outstanding issues with the firm, with the State Bar, and anything having to do with civil or criminal violations I may or may not have committed, on my own behalf and/or the firm's. He was extraordinarily comprehensive. The run-down took about 90 minutes, but I will boil it down for you.

As far as defending the firm and me in the Biotrimus matter was concerned, we would retain legal counsel while also keeping a watchful eye on the matter and the proceedings. He had called his old pal Dwight Benjamin of Benjamin, Bernard & Roth, as respected as a corporate defense lawyer in the country, and the retainer was being drawn up. Dad told me that Dwight said: "The dumb shit should've married her," and that he finds himself more and more disappointed in criminals. It may take some time, but he believed the firm and I would both ultimately be exonerated and/or removed as defendants or respondents in any and all proceedings, be they criminal or civil.

As far as my alleged ethical improprieties were concerned, the firm would represent me. He told me they had already begun negotiating with the Bar, who was hot to appear to scapegoat me without it being too painful for either the firm or me, and the result would be some kind of suspension, likely six months, which seemed harsh to me, but since disbarment had initially been on the table, this wasn't all that bad, or so Dad said.

As far as the firm was concerned, I would be suspended for that same six-month period without pay. I could barely hold back tears. Dad must've seen the look on my face and said: "Don't be such a pussy, Dale. Just keep listening," so I did. "I told you I was going to take care of you, so just pay attention. You can cry later."

He went on to say that Sherry and I needed to develop notes on every case I still had anything to do with. When that was done, I would be relieved of my keys to my prestigious parking space, and I was not to appear at the office unless asked to do so by an associate. I had braced myself for a certain amount of pain, but this was too much. "So, this is you taking care of me?"

"Dale, we have to make it look like we're taking this very seriously, and this kind of in-house reprimand, along with the suspension from the bar, will make things go better with the gigantic mess you've created with Biotrimus. Can you understand that?"

"Yeah, but…"

"No buts. This is part of the defense strategy. So, yes, this is me taking care of you: my son, my partner, my client, my codefendant, and everything we've built here. And don't worry: You're still a partner; you keep your office, you take an extended holiday, six months go by, and all is well. We may even have everything resolved by then. Probably not, but it's possible."

"The last part of it is, we want your spending to go cold. We've already got Eastman working the forensics on this, but it's unwieldy. You're not going to use your credit cards or the company expense account or cash anything out to survive. I've put half a million into an account with both our names on it that you can draw from over the next six months. You use the debit card; you write checks; you draw cash when you need it. Just that account. Ya' think you can live on $84K a month for the next six months?" he said, dripping with sarcasm.

I started to respond without really thinking. He stopped me and blasted me with his multi-million-dollar machine gun mouth: "It's a rhetorical question, schmuck. You cost all of us a great deal in terms of time and money, and this $500K is *my* money, so I don't wanna hear any more bullshit whining about whether I am taking care of you. *YOU* fucked up, and *WE* are covering *YOUR* ass. And remember: Humility, contrition, regret. You're the victim. Now, it is a fact that you kept your involvement in Biotrimus from everyone here, even Sherry. Correct?"

"Yeah."

"You are to admit to that at every turn. Understand? If I hear of you pulling away from that fact or even shading a little bit, you will be longing for the wrath of God soon after because you will first have to deal with the wrath of *me,* and there will be nothing left of you. This is *everything*. Do you understand me? You did this on your own and didn't say anything to anyone because you knew it was wrong. Like that, everything will work out fine. Without it, we're fucked. Not just you. And it's true, isn't it? So just tell the fucking truth?" he proclaimed with his great prosecutorial-speak.

Aside from the obvious, there was nothing for me to say: "I get it, Dad. I know you're right. It just doesn't feel very good."

"...You're about to take six months off. I'd like to take six months off! I think that would feel *very* good!"

"I'm sorry. You're right. Anything else, or should I just start in with Sherry?"

"Go. Come see me end-of-day," he ordered.

CHAPTER 19

Sea Change

During the few days of attending to all that was expected of me, I was a mess. I wasn't even trying to put on my Buddha Suit as if this solution was hiding somewhere in my consciousness. It's kind of like hiding something somewhere where you can find it later, but forgetting where you hid it.

Aside from Dwight Benjamin, a bigger-than-life heavyweight litigator with an orator's voice, who managed to get me to breathe easily for about half of the hour I spent with him in his office and believed that everything would turn out okay. I was actually wondering, projecting, and elaborating mischievously out loud how many lawyers in the country were screwing (not figuratively) their clients at that very moment. I felt no support from anyone at our offices besides Sherry—even my father, who was purportedly taking care of me.

Paranoid, depressed, anxiety-ridden, frightened, angry, desperate, lonely, overwhelmed, disconsolate: it's hard to think of a state of being, aside from peace, which did not last over and through me those few days. One of those evenings, after leaving the office, I was so discombobulated that I started yelling at a very old lady in front of me in line at a Ralphs in West LA simply for taking too long to pay because she was writing out a check.

I'm not a very young man myself, and I would normally be charmed by a character like this who is very polite. It might not have been so bad if she had yelled back and told me to fuck off, but I'd really terrified her. She started apologizing and shaking so badly that she couldn't write the check. It looked like she might start to cry, maybe even have some kind of medical emergency, so I left, presumably in a huff but fearing that someone might call the police.

Over those days, the negotiation with the Bar was also resolved, perhaps that quickly as another example of my father's engineering skills. I remember noting that this idea of concurrent suspensions would look very tidy, legally, but I couldn't help resenting it anyway. Swift justice, as they say, along with sentences served concurrently. And so, on that Friday, after having been put through the wringer and touching base with everyone to make sure I was good to go, I put some of my things in a box, left my office keys and parking lot clicker with Sherry and was on my way out the door just past 3 p.m.

Sherry was reassuring: "Don't worry, Dale. Everything's gonna be fine." By then, I was well into the zombie zone alluded to above, yet somehow managed to say the right thing: "Thanks, Sherry. You've been great. Please stay on top of things and let me know if anyone needs anything from me; anything at all."

It was true. She had been great. But what I really wanted at that moment was to somehow have a Uzi in the box, pull it out, and massacre everyone in the place except for Sherry. She'd been the only one who was more than halfway decent to me through this whole ordeal and went out of her way to remain kind, even though I'd probably been a difficult boss all along.

I didn't know what to do with myself, so I drove straight home. Todd was there. Todd didn't drink or get stoned anymore at all, but I decided that that was the exact thing for me to do and got out the bong, some weed, and cracked open a Sierra Brew. He didn't even blink. Never judgmental or critical, he really was my saving grace. I might have thrown him out just then if he'd tried to stop me.

Looking back, I realize he literally never got fed up with me or, at least, never seemed to. He just listened, understood, and had truly wise input to offer. Coming from our family, it is a relatively gargantuan mystery where he got this kind of patience. There is also that core fact in our relationship: though we'd gone our separate ways back when he left us all for good, he left me behind as well. He knows I never stopped loving him, and I know he never stopped loving me, either.

Todd got wind of my six-month time out as he was on speaking terms with the folks now—just kept them at a distance: "Listen, Bro, it's time to take the trip."

"What, ya got some acid?"

"Do you really think I've brought LSD, and that's what I'm suggesting, ya bonehead?"

"Alright, sorry, I'm a little wacky right now. What? What trip?"

"Sail down the coast. Surf, fish, dive. Go ashore as we please. All the way to Colombia. No time.

As long as it takes."

And right then and there, my clever brother—always full of surprises and probably inspired by the second-hand smoke—stood up to throw down some Shakespeare from *The Tempest*, and nailed it:

Full fathom five thy father lies;
Of his bones are coral made;
Those are pearls that were his eyes:
Nothing of him that doth fade,
But doth suffer a sea-change
Into something rich and strange.
Sea-nymphs hourly ring his knell:
Ding-dong.
Hark! now I hear them,—ding-dong, bell.

Ding-dong! A sea change. Yes. I doubt that I can sufficiently express in words the wave of thought and emotion that hit me in response to these words, but I will try. At first, my stream-of-consciousness was absolutely waylaid by what felt like a thousand reasons why this idea was completely out of the question. If I hadn't been sitting down, I might have passed out. I think I almost went insane. I couldn't decide what to say because I had a thousand things to say all at once. God knows what I looked like to Todd as I gaped at him and around the living room, dumbfounded. Ding-dong bell.

After a while, I tried to begin to say something several times and realized it was BS. Todd was saying nothing, just looking at me, taking a bong hit to stall for time. Todd remained silent; I guess knowing he had run my ding-dong bell. I took another bong hit with one hand and, with the other, drank my beer to stall for more time, then through the haze, woke up to the fact that Todd was right and that this was very likely the best thing I could possibly do with my life right then. And if he wanted to do it with me, that was an even greater blessing.

Finally, after at least five minutes, though I really don't know, I said: "Ya know, what they said to Einstein, right?"

"No, what?"

"You're a genius."

Of course, as reckless as it may sound, a trip like this requires planning. It also requires a sailboat. As we began to shop and put the whole thing together, Todd and I became, I'd say, a bit too giddy with excitement for public consumption. Adding to the fun, hilariously enough, my father was all for the idea: I was relatively incommunicado for several months, just so long as I was willing to check in on a regular basis sounded just right to him, the partners, and Benjamin, as well.

We got a little frustrated at first, looking for the right boat. What we initially saw was either unreasonably expensive or perhaps not quite seaworthy. Then, a stroke of genius—we decided to look into restoring "Demurrer," Poppa's old sailboat. It was kept at the bottom, clean, and under general maintenance so it wouldn't look like an eyesore at its slip in the Marina. We didn't want to sell it for nostalgic reasons and the effort in listing it and dealing with it. So it was just sitting there, sometimes used for an occasional Sunday brunch or if we happened to be in the area with time on our hands, both of which were very rare.

So, we called Dad to see if we could restore it and use it for our sailing adventures. He chuckled and said, "Be my guest," probably just thinking we weren't going to go through with it.

For a 50+ year old sailboat, Demurrer was in pretty decent shape, with all the bells and whistles from twenty-five years ago. It had pretty much what we would need and want for the journey: GPS, a spacious galley, custom bedding, Surround Sound speakers, satellite TV, beautifully appointed throughout two comfortable cabins, and a full john/head; it was perfect for two guys sailing into somewhat treacherous waters.

So we hired the right experts to rebuild the motor, update all the wiring to marine grade standards, and install a new solar energy system. We recovered the cushions, got a new navigation system, repaired the sails, and added some new appliances, such as a bigger freezer and refrigerator. We also updated the gear that required it to put in a great new entertainment center. When all was said and done, I spent almost $75, 000 but we had a classic sold sailboat with all the state-of-the-art systems. It looked and sailed beautifully.

As Dad insisted, we registered the boat in both our names to handle any legal ramifications and joyously continued planning. Effectively, Dad had given us an advance on our inheritance as he lost his interest in sailing many years ago after his father passed away. I rented my house for a five-month stint via Craigslist to a screenwriter who was coming out from New York on a studio gig. He was bringing his wife and baby. It felt good to be renting to a young family. Hell, at that point, I was feeling good about almost everything. Also, though the property was momentarily compromised because of the litigation in process, I still had all that equity in it, so there was going to be some nice passive income coming in while we loped along the coast.

Todd chose not to capitalize on it, but he had a lot of equity in his house, too, and owned the building where his studio was located. He just handed over the keys to some artist friends. The deal was that they had actual projects to develop and complete within a timeframe. He incorporated a nonprofit and hired an administrator. I was impressed and not a little ashamed about my profit motive.

We were just bursting with enthusiasm in those last few days before we left. Even the anxiety was enjoyable. We'd been sailing since we were kids and had boned up on our terrific new ship, so we were comfortable with that aspect of it. All the licensing had been taken care of, and our passports were in order. We'd familiarized ourselves with the latest navigation tools. We'd said our goodbyes to whoever we had to say them to and made arrangements for being gone indefinitely. Indeed, we were ready to go two days before we were scheduled to shove off.

It was also kinda strange in the sense that there was all that excitement and planning, along with all the weight of what I'd been going through, as well as some really fine little trips around the South Bay and up to Malibu to get used to the vessel and the wind.

Then, one day, we set sail on the fully restored Demurrer's maiden voyage, just after breakfast as if it were just another day. It seemed like another day as we set out, but it was a new beginning. I suppose it wasn't so for Todd, but I felt free for the first time in my life. Just Todd and I were on the open sea, going where we wanted to go and where the wind blew us; no expectations, no schedule, no time beyond day and night. The time became now.

The sea changes into something rich and strange.

CHAPTER 20

Journey of a Lifetime

We set sail on a Wednesday morning in May for the simple reason that we were ready and the time had come. Also, as planned, it would be a full moon that night. It was a beautiful day for sailing, with offshore winds powering us out of the Santa Monica Bay, where we expected to hook into those reliable, perfect northwest winds—the Pacific Ocean Superhighway.

Todd had been contemplating what to do with Paloma: his sweet, pretty, four-year-old chocolate Labrador mixed with God knows what. He decided to take her with us on the trip.

At first, I hesitated. I know it's horrible to admit, but I never really liked dogs much. When we were kids, our mother had a couple of nasty little miniature poodles that she doted over. These were not our family dogs. They didn't care much for anyone other than our mother—who embarrassingly coddled them—and each other: their own little Gang of Three. I also had a Doberman Pinscher chase me down the block and bite me once, literally bit my ass, then tackled me, attempting to maul me a while until the macho owner came running up to yank the dog off me—a child. So, I guess these bits of childhood trauma made me pause and wonder if it would be too much of a hassle to have a dog alone who might turn on me.

Then I was made to remember that I'd been hanging out with Paloma since Todd came back into my life, that she was a loving, playful, wonderful dog who loved the water and also had this weirdly wise look about her—a personality, and personality is important. I realized I'd be very happy to have her aboard.

In discussing whether to dog or not to dog, he saw me hesitate: "Dale, you love Paloma," he said calmly, and it snapped me out of it. That was all it took. She and Todd were inseparable. As our journey progressed, their bond and love spread out to include me. We bought one of those plastic pet-potty things that look like a tiny patch of grass so she could go comfortably when we were out at sea—easy to set up and clean up after.

We were ready, so it only took us about an hour to prepare. Then, we motored out of the harbor. I had always been fascinated by sailboats leaving any harbor, wondering who was on board, where they were going, and how sailing affected their lives. Now, it was us.

Demurrer had a good Yanmar rebuilt diesel in her, and we were confident we could pull through just about any chop, swell, or current. Once out of the harbor, a strong wind was gusting from the northwest. We hoisted the mainsail and unfurled the jib, and it was smooth sailing downwind—Mexico bound.

We shut off the motor and had a nice downwind run. The boat was keeling nicely on the starboard tack. After a short while, a calm feeling came over me. Whatever anxieties and troubles I had as we set off eased away then, as if leaving the harbor in a literal sense. Seeing the hills and the place I grew up fading away slowly like that allowed me to leave all my attachments to those troubles behind as well.

Southern Cross by Crosby, Stills, Nash, and Young, The Beach Boys' *Sloop John B*, and *Come Sail Away* by Styx filled my head. *Sailing* by Christopher Cross cropped in, and I swotted it away, advancing to the next song in my inner iPod. Once, I got in a groove and felt the ocean waves Sail Away by Enya playing in my inner speakers. It was beautiful, moody, and perfect for a night watch. *Avalon* by Roxy Music played next. It isn't really a sailing song, but it's a beautiful song. I have always been associated with sailing because of the crossing to Avalon Harbor on Catalina, which is also a great song for a night watch. For a moment, I wondered if my inner Buddha guided my inner music choices to help me get into The Priceless Techniques.

When you lose sight of land, your perspective changes, allowing you to look inward and connect to life itself. Minutes faded into hours until time stood still. The only talk between Todd and me during those first few hours was all technical and very moment-to-moment. We were simply sailing, continuing to get to know the boat, Paloma alternating from cheering us on to laying out even more calm and tranquil than we were. As my cares drifted and faded astern, Todd and I shared knowing glances and the thrill and dreaminess of beginning.

After this initial, exquisite run, we began to talk freely as the journey unfolded. I could feel myself opening up, physically feeling areas of my body letting go. Even the sound of my laughter was noticeably different, heartier.

We had stocked plenty of provisions in our brand-new large freezer, ranging from necessities to indulgences. We had the basics: potable water, rice, pasta, instant soups, cans of chili, soup, beans, vegetables, and, of course, dog food. No SpaghettiOs or Top Ramen. Rather, we had a Costco run gathering frozen fruit, vegetables, cheese, ice cream/popsicles, frozen quality grass-fed beef, and other quality "organic" meat. Fresh meat, vegetables, fruit, Greek yogurt, nut milk, and nut butter were in the fridge, and some grass fed ground beef, hot dogs, and free range ground chicken were in the freezer if we got tired of fresh tuna and lobster. Also, there was a nice collection of healthy dark chocolate and select tasty morsels for our sweet palate. Indeed, we'd overstocked the animal protein. We hoped to rely on fishing and whatever bounty we could gain from the ocean for that, but it seemed smart to have a backup, just in case we didn't live up to romantic notions of ourselves as ocean-going hunter-gatherers.

As the sun set that first day at sea and the night crept up, we could not have been more pleased. The moon was up before we noticed it, reflecting brilliantly on the surface of the ocean. By the time the dusk faded, the stars blazed away, diamonds in our eyes.

We sailed through the starry, clear night, taking turns at the helm in order to get as far along as possible. We did have a new fancy autopilot system, but if we sailed at night, one of us had to stay awake just to make sure we stayed out of harm's way—everything from loose containers to smuggler's boats to freighters. Again, it is pleasant to romanticize ancient seafarers such as the Phoenicians, the Vikings, and the Pacific Islanders and talk about the constellations being our guide. That talk was fine and good, but we were aware of our limitations and relied heavily on our GPS system.

We were headed for Mexico, not the Marshall Islands: Cabo, not the Cooks.

In the morning, we crossed the border into Mexico and made it down to Rosarito Beach by late that afternoon. The waves were perfect and challenging: big, overhead, and fast, with a light offshore wind reeling down the point at K38. We dropped anchor not far offshore. Another blessing: there were only a few people out. I was raring to go, but Todd insisted we meditate before setting out.

We sat on the foam pads on deck that we'd brought for just this purpose. Todd guided us through meditation for a few minutes, and then we sat in Savasana for another fifteen in silence, the gentle ocean washing under us like in a dream.

Todd grabbed his board, told Paloma to watch the boat, jumped into the water, paddled over, and made his way into the lineup. As eager as I was twenty minutes earlier, I'd somehow become nervous. The surf didn't look too dangerous, but it was a fast wave over a cobblestone reef. For whatever reason, I had a gaping pit in my stomach. I was looking at the rocks on the shore and the few guys who were there ripping. I couldn't pinpoint where this fear was coming from; it felt like more than one thing. I'd surfed waves like this before, and I was tranquil as can be coming out of our meditation, but it was reeling fast down the line at about eighteen-second intervals. It took some effort, but I finally got up the nerve to paddle my way into the lineup.

I sat on my board a bit outside, pretending to give the other surfers the respect they truly deserved since they appeared to be seasoned, hardcore surfers trading waves. But really, I was still afraid. I watched them take off and how the wave broke. Watching them gave me the confidence to at least try, so I made my way into the pack and was ready to surf.

On my first few waves, I struggled to paddle in and either pulled back or didn't make it in because I wasn't able to get up enough speed or angle off the shoulder. Then, I paddled too far in front of a wave and embarrassingly tumbled over the falls. Luckily, I was with Todd, my apologist, who was tearing it up, so these guys didn't look at me quite as funny as they might have. Toward the end of the session, I was able to establish some rhythm and paddle into some nice inside waves, get to my feet (albeit slowly), and get in some decent rides. It was a satisfying end to what was mostly kind of a bummer.

After a couple of hours, we paddled, I'd say, about 150 yards back to the boat, and, man, was I spent. My arms were so sore that it was a struggle to climb the ladder onto the boat, and I collapsed on the deck. Paloma was barking at us, perhaps laughing at me, along with Todd, who was definitely laughing at me. Todd made some more coffee, chopped up a pineapple, and we ate it with some Greek yogurt. He gave Paloma some water and fed her. I laughed too after a while, and my exhaustion gave way to that physical sense of ease I'd felt come over my body the day before as if my body was remembering it.

We hung out in the evening, bathed, and watched the sunset. My, it was a fine time. We considered locking up the boat and taking the dinghy ashore to find a restaurant in that part of town, but our conversation took us along well into the night, and it felt unnecessary to leave. We talked about The Three Priceless Techniques and resolved to do our best to act as if we were Buddhas on the path, look out at the world as if it were one *Buddha Field* after another, and see others as if they were Buddhas on the path. Just talking about it made it more and more so.

At some point that night, I remembered us causing trouble on Grampa's boat as real little kids and him catching us at it, but instead of being mad, he smiled at us and joined in our mischief. I got a bit lost in the reverie and had pulled into an almost dreamlike state about it, to the degree that when Todd spoke again, it startled me. I related the memory, and he remembered it, too. An exquisite smile flashed across his face, and both of us sat there grinning from ear to ear. I thought Poppa might be watching over us just then and that he might come along for the ride, a kind of angel taking care of us as our trip unfolded.

We had countless blissful, starry, starry nights like that. Usually around sunset, whether on the move or not, one of us would fire up the barbecue strapped to the stanchions. We'd do some prep work and get to cooking. After dinner, Todd would strum his guitar or ukulele and sing or both. Sometimes, he would play along with the music on the sound system.

Todd's life had been consumed by music. As kids, he introduced me to all the classic rock—the Stones, Pink Floyd, Led Zeppelin, the Beatles, and Neil Young. He was an intuitive musician and could learn and play instruments naturally. Sometimes, I would join in on the other guitar. Sometimes, he played alone, and sometimes, we would simply listen to the sound of the ocean and the birds without any music. Just talking with the ocean around us, waves lapping gently against the boat—it was a beautiful thing.

As a child, our parents insisted we take piano lessons, and the very strict German teacher, Ms. Schmidt, would come over every Saturday morning for years. My lesson would be the 1st hour, and I would dutifully study and practice. Todd, who had tremendous talent, would be resistant to doing lessons, let alone practice, but could play his own music on the piano, so we both had the basic musical education at a young age.

There was enough room for all three of us to sleep in the V-berth. Often, we'd just drift off to sleep in the cockpit or wherever we lay comfortably in our spacious ocean home. Todd, though in an informal mode, was training me. Sometimes late at night, he would get a just-right tone going, mild and hypnotic, and talk about the chakras or read from some translation of a Tibetan Buddhist tract. I'm sure I didn't understand all of it, but there was osmosis taking place, and I couldn't help but feel his wisdom seeping into me, or so it seemed.

Todd was an insatiable reader of anything New Age or spiritual. Anything written by spiritual leaders. His favorite was the classic *Way of the Peaceful Warrior* by Dan Millman. He also enjoyed books by Gary Zuckoff and Deepak Chopra and embraced their teachings.

The meditation practice I'd rejected early on was now something I had grown to love as part of our daily ritual: twice and sometimes three times a day. As I got better at it, the nuisance, pain, and grief of it turned into a practice I looked forward to. Suddenly, I could meditate for an hour, and it would go by in what seemed like maybe fifteen blissful minutes. It was cozy, floating in the middle of the ocean, and easy to breathe in and breathe out.

Time drifted by until we stopped paying attention to it. No, never mind. After that, we were simply rolling down the coast. One morning, after an amazingly deep sleep, I woke up, and, per usual, we did a little yoga and meditated together. This time, though, going into the meditation, I fell very quickly into a deep state, with brilliant sprays of color entering my mind's eye. I saw purples, blues, greens, and oranges, but at first, I did not really understand them. Then, all of a sudden, at that moment, The Three Priceless Techniques became very clear to me. It was almost as powerful as when I had the visitations with the Buddha back at my house, but there was no Buddha this time. It was as if these ideas and states of being were not merely available to me; they were getting inside me and setting up shop in my soul.

We made our way down to Ensenada and docked at the Coral Marina Hotel. We went ashore to stock up on provisions and spend some time on dry land—Paloma, too. In fact, we found a chic groomer, and she had a fine two hours at the spa, all fresh and clean when she came out, wagging her tail and her entire body uncontrollably, smelling better than we did (as opposed to two hours earlier). We spent those two hours at the Marina Grill, eating *pollo a la parrilla* (delicious Mexican-style grilled chicken), drinking Tiger Woods, which the new generation calls lemonade and iced tea, and taking in the splendor.

Drinking for Todd was an odd alchemy of some very refined juice combos. Once we got Pali back, we made our way to a local farmer's market and then to a supermarket, checked everything off our list, and got ourselves and our supplies back on board and stowed away. Time to figure out our next surf spot. We decided to make our way to Scorpion Bay. As Google Maps flies, what was about sixteen hours by road was around 540 miles by sea and a couple of days sailing on the open sea in deep waters.

Over those few days, I dreamed vividly and intensely, sleeping more often than at any other time during the trip: Either outside on the cushions under the starry night or in the V-Berth with the hatch open, drifting off into a blessed state of unconsciousness. Some people count sheep, and I count shooting stars. And counting my blessings.

Strangely, though, when I woke up after those naps, I'd invariably have an anxious urge to work, to get something done, not on the boat but as a lawyer. Then I'd realize there was no work or responsibility of that kind to be taken care of, and a surge of warmth and ease would rush through me. That knee-jerk reaction to make money was leaving me.

My father would not be pleased. Or maybe he'd be envious.

We arrived at Scorpion Bay and docked outside the Third Point at Ponga Beach since this was supposed to be the best spot. We arrived to find that Desert Point throbbing with one of those juicy, powerful, spring southern hemisphere swells that had originated deep in the Roaring Forties, south of Australia.

The northern hemisphere springs fall in the southern hemisphere. Summer diminishes the Antarctic ice pack, so the winds have a longer *fetch* to blow over and kick up ground swells that carry a shocking amount of energy across the equator and all the way up deep into the northern hemisphere. As Google Maps flies, that's around 7000 miles from below New Zealand to Scorpion Bay. The longer a swell travels through the open ocean, the more orderly and powerful it becomes, and the wavelength increases, an indication of power.

That's what was happening when we approached Scorpion Bay: clearly, this was a high-quality, spring southern hemisphere swell. We could see it and feel the power under the boat. Quality energy.

"Man overboard!" Todd yelled giddily, grabbing his 6'6" Al Merrick Flyer and jumping out of the boat. I was, again, a tad reluctant to paddle out. The point was striped with overhead waves. "Corduroy to the horizon" is the poetic surfer description: gargantuan creases in gigantic corduroy pants, one after the other, at eighteen-second intervals.

Eventually, the thought pushed me overboard: "What kind of a pussy are you?"

I grabbed the Anderson 9'0 "Marshall Brothers" longboard and paddled gamely over to the lineup. By the time I got to the top of Third Point, Todd had already gotten himself inside and was having a blast. He was tearing it up, and I'd be lying if I didn't admit to feeling envious. I also got some stink eye from some kids who weren't about to take any shit from some ol' man until they saw that I could actually surf, which I found funny at first since I was that kinda kid once—funny until it wasn't.

After an hour of catching some fun peelers, I became complacent. I paddled into a set wave, but I didn't fully commit. I heard a voice yell, "Get off my wave, geezer!" just before my face hit the water. I crashed into the guy and wiped us both out. On the way down, my hand got caught between our boards on impact, and underwater, I was pretty sure I'd fractured my wrist or worse. When I surfaced, I looked around for the kid to apologize; I was also a little worried he and his buds might come after me. But no one was close to me, and I felt awkward. I should have found them and bought his whole crew dinner, but I was so wounded—emotionally along with the wrist—I paddled back to the boat, ashamed, feeling like a complete loser. I got myself aboard and was now at home enough to attend to the violent pain in my arm and hand. Like a hurt child, I just wanted to go home. I felt sorry for myself, which triggered an array of thoughts about everything going wrong back home, leading to the vehement conclusion: I certainly DO NOT want to go home!

And again, the question: "What kind of a coward are you?" I managed to stop the downward spiral, regroup, and begin a meditation. Seeing those twenty-year-old rippers as Buddhas on the Path wasn't that hard, so I went with it in the meditation and felt better. Paloma and I were sitting together placidly when Todd popped onto the boat about an hour later: stoked. It startled me for a moment because I was in a Zen state before I realized it was him. He was a bit too high on life just then to get bummed about my experience.

Through his sly grin: "Why, Mr. Congeniality, there you are!" he quipped.

Then he saw my wrecked Anderson board: "That's a sad sight. Listen, Dale, we're lucky that kid wasn't hurt. His pals wanted to kick your ass, but he cooled them out. He was pretty funny, referring to you as The Senior Surfer. Oh, they'll be mocking you for days."

"I'm glad he's okay. Luckily, I didn't break my wrist. It's just twisted or somethin'. I'm such a dork. Maybe I need a lesson."

"Nah. Hang in there, bud. You'll be fine. Just gotta find your flow and feel the rhythm of the wave, and you will. Hang in there."

We got dinner together. Todd very rarely ate steak, but he said he was up for it that morning, so we pulled two of them out of the freezer before surfing to allow them to thaw out. He seasoned them after he finished toying with me about the day's mishaps. The New York cuts went well with some of the broccoli and carrots we'd gotten at the Ensenada farmers' market, which we also grilled. Paloma was uber-stoked to be the recipient of our table scraps—mostly fat. We'd bought some nice avocados and red onions, so we sliced them up and dressed them in olive oil, lemon, apple cider vinegar, sea salt, and cayenne pepper. No wine for me, just another refreshing Tiger Woods. Another beautiful sunset and the slosh of the water again made my painful day fade pleasantly into the night, rest, and sleep—the wrist remarkably better after a good meal.

We spent another day at Scorpion Bay, and Todd continued having a ball in the waves. Sure enough, I had to weather those kids lightheartedly mocking me: The Senior Surfer: "Hey, watch out; here comes Senior Surfer, he'll mow you down!" and "Looks like seniors' day, fellas, we better pack it in," and "Is 'that a surfboard or a wheelchair?" I took it with a grain of salt. I guess I deserved it. I understood these were just college kids having a good time, although this was not very *Buddha-like* of them! Or was it? My wrist was sore but improving. I continued to struggle with the waves, but I did get some decent rides. One was a set wave: I waited patiently outside, gathered up my courage, stroked into it at the right spot, set up my bottom turn, and kicked out all the way down at the next point. So, I felt pretty good about that.

We had another beautiful evening and night on the boat, Todd putting together a gorgeous salad. We set sail, heading south in the morning without much of an agenda. We knew we wanted to get all the way down to Cabo San Lucas on this leg.

As Google Flies, we were eight hours plus and 336 miles on the proper road from San Juanico to Cabo, over 300 miles, and a couple of days by sea.

CHAPTER 21

The Calm before the Storm

Grandpa Owen taught us the saying when we were very young: "Red sky at night, sailor's delight. Red sky in the morning, sailor take warning." Such wisdom proved true on the way from Scorpion Bay to Cabo, and we blew it.

We had a calm, clear night, followed by a morning with red, turbulent skies—but we didn't take warnings despite the weather forecast of possible storms. We were too far along to turn back when we saw the storm clouds later that day, and we decided to take our chances and cut through the storm. First, it began to rain; then, it really started to pour. Rough seas, and we were a bit too far from shore for comfort. When we saw those red skies that morning, we should have found a secure, protected cove to pull into. That became our goal pretty quickly, but we were irresponsibly late on that decision, then too brash. Then, we were too deep in it: howling winds and open ocean waves knocked us around wildly.

We took turns at the helm so each one of us could be dry and fresh. We were looking for a safe place to pull into, but this stretch of Baja is not easy. The movies the previous owner had given us came in handy that day. I watched parts of The Marx Brothers' *Day at the Races*. Talk about *Buddha Fields* and Buddhas on the Path! And Surrealists, to boot!

We reefed the sails and strapped in so we wouldn't fall overboard. We put Paloma below in the Galley. She was sliding around down there, not knowing what was going on.

Yet, those massive ocean rollers were bumpy and scary at times. There was no respite and nothing we could do until we came across the right cove or passed the storm. At one point, my emotions got the best of me: waves of fear, anxiety, and whatever else were throwing me around like the waves throwing us around in the water. I wondered what kind of life I would have when I returned to LA. I thought about leaving the United States altogether. I thought about how my parents would react if Todd and I were lost at sea. Then the cabin door blasted open, the whole wet world chiming in.

"You're up, Dale!"

"Okay! Be up in a minute."

Todd went back to the helm while I went down below to regroup. Paloma looked a little nervous, but I reassured her: "Don't worry, girl. We'll be just fine," although I wasn't so sure myself. I joined Todd on deck, and he yelled that we were looking for the right cove and that even if something looked really good, we needed to keep our eye on the depth finder to make sure we didn't hit something on our way in. I should call him if I see something good.

"You cool?" he asked. I nodded, and he went below. I was scared, but the fear gave way after a while to the beauty of the moment, and I knew we were going to be okay. Then I laughed at myself, wondering how many sailors had the same thought before wrecking the ship and drowning at sea. Strangely, I was better at running the boat between the waves than surfing. I guess that set of old skills ran deeper inside me than the other.

After a half-hour or so, we did come across what looked like somewhere we could get in and drop anchor. I called out to Todd, and he came up to check it out. He agreed we should try, so we sped up the motor, let her warm up for a few minutes, and turned toward the shore.

There is always the danger of running aground along the Pacific Coast when coming in from out at sea, and we had to be careful. The depth finder functioned nicely for us, directing us away from both points of the cove and also away from a rocky part of it near the northwest point.

We got in deep enough to drop anchor out of the high winds and waves and began working in the cabin, drying up the wet spots and trying to make things cozy for the three of us to eat, hang out, and finally call it a night. The wind howled, and the boat rocked, but nothing like when we were out on the open ocean.

The storm passed after a few hairy hours. Things were damp, but after we got out of our wet clothes, dried off, and changed, we could mellow out a bit. Paloma was very glad to get toweled down this time, which is not always the case. The heater kept us nice and warm. We were tired, of course, but we also felt an overwhelming sense of relief that we had pulled through.

Todd agreed again to a meal involving other-than-fish animal protein, and I joked with him over franks and beans that I was turning him back into a carnivore. We hadn't talked much about LA on that trip, but we did that night. It felt ominous enough to be happy about moving *away* from instead of *toward* the place. We all fell asleep in the V-berth, warm and dry. I had a good feeling that we were taking care of each other as I drifted off to sleep—that we were a fine crew.

CHAPTER 22

Baja California Dreamin'

We awoke to a brilliant sunrise the following morning. It was so magnificent—the colors of the ocean and sky so solid yet stark, while the water was so calm that it made the previous day's storm feel like a dream. Or was this the dream? Either way, we felt renewed. Yes, I believe *Pali* did too. I fed her and made some coffee. Then, we meditated by ourselves with coffee. All alone in that unknown cove, having come through the night and then finding ourselves quite at home and at peace in the world, we had quite a blissful morning.

Todd noticed some sweet little waves breaking off the north point. It was a place that had to be accessed by boat or mountain goat. We grabbed the longboards and paddled over as the surf picked up with an incoming tide to groove on these perfect little 3-4-foot-plus rollers for a couple of hours. Perhaps the offshore winds were blown by the Buddha himself to add some groomed perfection and lead us toward enlightenment. When you are lucky enough to ride flawless waves alone in a wild setting, you remember how damned much fun surfing is. It occurred to me that this must mean that I really am old now: The Senior Surfer, as it were, but I didn't care. I was too busy beaming before, during, and after each ride.

We paddled back to the boat, dried off, and changed. We broke out the fishing tackle, got it together, and cast out our lines. I caught a couple of groupers, but we threw them back because they were too small. Within an hour, Todd reeled in a beautiful halibut after a moderate fight by a skilled fisherman. I estimated it to be about eighteen to twenty pounds, which was more than enough for the time being. We were overjoyed.

In my head, I made a list of My Top Five Fish: 1. Branzino. 2. Halibut. 3. Chilean sea bass. 4. Salmon. 5. Bluefin tuna. My tongue started touching my lips, reacting to the vision of these delights in my head. I briefly wondered how the Buddha might reply to this vision, but I didn't want to think about that right now…

Todd cleaned the fish, cut up some big filets, packed and put some of them in the freezer, sliced another up real thin, sashimi-style, dousing it with lemon, cayenne, good sea salt, and fresh chopped cilantro, which made for a terrific snack right away.

We marinated the two filets we'd saved for dinner in olive oil, lemon, salt, fresh ground pepper, and cilantro and put them in the fridge to grill later, turning them every little while in the marinade. Then we got the grill going. When we grilled the fish, we also grilled what was left of our fresh vegetables since they were on their last leg. I worked my way through that over the next few hours as we looked over the boat to see how she'd fared through the storm. We were alive and happy.

Eating so clean felt so satisfying. I was changing my eating habits to be more like Todd, single ingredients, not processed with additives, particularly sugar or its substitute—as close to farm-to-table as possible. My drinking and pot smoking subsided, too, as I was emerging physically in the fittest and most authentic version of myself that I kept envisioning, knowing it was absolutely up to me to transform my body and health. The healthier and leaner I became, the easier it was for me to be the man I wanted to be mentally, spiritually, and physically.

Later that day, we felt blessed to witness a majestic sight: a pod of gray whales making their way up north. I'd never seen so many at one time: such grace and ease in their natural migratory habitat. A primal awe and joy came over me, the high point of a magnificent day. We stayed another night in that blessed cove and pushed off in the morning.

There was no wind, so we slowly motored south and came across a little fishing village where we could get some basic supplies, including fuel. I guess those villagers didn't see many tourists. They seemed fascinated by us. They were so friendly, though we weren't sure if they were laughing with us or at us. They also gave us some tips about navigating down the coast to our next stop, Magdalena Bay, and sold us their favorite bait and some homemade lures. Todd speaks solid California surfer busboy Spanglish, which smoothed transactions countless times throughout the trip. He'd traveled enough through Mexico, Central and South America, and Spain to have it down. Back on the boat, still not sure if they were laughing with us or at us, we fueled up, put our goods away, and set sail. We motored off into the night at a nice, even pace.

CHAPTER 23

Uncharted Territories

The wind picked up after a while, and we were able to sail through the night and most of the next day all the way to majestic Magdalena Bay, a pristine point break on a remote peninsula across from Loreto, a touristy fishing town on the Sea of Cortez. Todd had been there before and knew about a camp run by an affable US ex-pat named Steve—though *affable* sells him short. He was a magnanimous spirit! We anchored offshore and rowed to Steve's beach. He saw us coming, greeted us, remembered Todd, and invited us onsite to hang out with the campers and share some meals.

After we were introduced to whoever was around—being that Cabo was So Cal to the South—I felt a little terror that there'd be someone I knew. Worse yet, an LA attorney I'd have to talk the talk with. I was wonderfully relieved that there was not, then trading stories sitting around on the beach; we spent the rest of the day with a handful of the group hiking up the mountain behind Fred's compound.

At the mountain peak, it was a clear day with vast ocean vistas for miles. The seven of us meditated together—eight if we include *Pali,* though I can't say for sure about her meditating. She was having a great day, though, and seemed pretty high when we concluded! We were all high. There is something powerful about group meditation that is not like meditating alone, which happened at that peak. We brought it down the hill with us, too: no drugs required.

Appetites inspired, we had fresh steamed lobster with drawn butter, black beans, white rice, and Fred's should-be-famous coleslaw for dinner. What Fred is most famous for is the sizeable tent (legend has it that the Red Hot Chili Peppers, also avid Malibu surfers, had played under that tent) he has set up as a music studio, filled with a terrific set

of instruments: acoustic and electric guitars, an electric bass, and a stand-up with a pick-up you can clip onto that acoustic bass. A few different kinds of keyboards, a very cool Gretsch silver sparkle drum set, and an incredible slew of percussion instruments, horns, reeds, mics, etc., along with amps and a damn good PA system. It was mostly a rock scene, so Todd and I could join in seamlessly. We were all up late jammin' a whole lotta Zeppelin, Stones, Dylan, Hendrix, etc., all night.

Fred was a great musician. He trained one of his workers to lay down some bass grooves, and Fred could sing.

A barely twenty-year-old local kid sat in, burning up a Les Paul. It was a great night, and Fred was a spectacular host. I remember thinking it funny that, after too many beers and my fair share of the smoke, it seemed incredibly chic to stumble out of the tent and pass out on the beach. Obviously, Todd played it straight and stayed up later. Smashed, I missed the sun coming up over the mountain, but I'd had a great night and woke up refreshed—that much drink and smoke notwithstanding.

When I did wake up, the morning was immediately surreal. I noticed right away that I was happy. It is fair to say that I had already been happy many times along the way on this trip, but it was always for some reason. There were times meditating when I was at peace with the world, and that was all quite real to me, but it was still the result of an act. That morning, I was happy for no reason at all. I was already in a bathing suit, so I removed my shirt and entered the ocean.

It was womb-like. That sweet stretch of beach and the mild conditions added up to such a blissful at-home-in-the-world feeling that I found myself laughing with glee in the water. Everywhere I looked was a *Buddha Field*. I flopped around for a while, swam here and swam there, and did a little body surfing, not a care in the world. I'd finally escaped into the deeper reality of the present moment, and the insight that came with it was that trying to do that and get there kills it to begin with. The seeker continues to seek. It is the seer who sees. Some time passed, and it felt like I should get back on the land, so I came in.

The swell came up overnight. We could hear it and feel it, which is a sound and feeling surfers love. We were glamping on the cliff and were lulled to sleep with sweet dreams of what was coming the next day. And the next day, I lived up to the dream: perfect, glassy, overhead right-handers in 70-degree water. Surfing by yourself is not fun, and surfing in crowds is not fun. But surfing with one or two other people you like or love is a blast. When you experience good waves with a minimal crowd, you remember that surfing is a lot of fun when you take out the frustration of dealing with other surfers. I felt good, I felt loose, and I surfed unselfconsciously. It was the best day I'd had in quite a while.

Surfers call it *stoke.* Only a surfer knows the feeling. I was feeling it.

Breakfast was served in the main house in the dining room: eggs how you wanted 'em, rice and beans, handmade corn tortillas, guacamole, salsa, and *queso fresco*. It was *huevos rancheros* but separated on the plate, fantastically prepared, with coffee and juice from the oranges in Fred's own grove. Also, an assortment of fresh fruit. Here, as well, I was not trying to see these folks as Buddhas on the path. They already were. I don't believe I had ever felt this brand of happiness before in my life, nor that I had ever had a natural smile on my face for such an extended period.

We were invited to stay, but it was such a fine day for sailing, we decided to shove off. We said our warm goodbyes to these great new friends that we might never see again. It had been so intensely beautiful it was hard to believe we'd only been there about eighteen hours.

Steve knew how to fortify sailors for a few days at sea. In exchange, we gave him a few bucks and supplies. We still had some decent stock on the boat, complemented with coffee, a dozen fresh eggs, avocados, cheese, tortillas, and salsa to repeat at sea the terrific breakfast we'd had that morning. Also, two live lobsters in a bucket of ocean water and some fresh fruits and vegetables from the farm were on the ready.

Steve gave us fuel. When I hugged him, I whispered in his ear that I'd like to send him a check when I got back to LA and asked him if 500 bucks would do. Half-expecting him to say no, followed by something wise about money, he said, *Sure,* and handed me a card from his pocket. "You can send it to this address," and we laughed about it as we started walking down to our dinghy.

"Fair enough," I said. "Though you're gambling that we'll live."

We set sail and had some nice prevailing winds. The next few days were smooth sailing and smooth living. We felt like it was more than just the wind at our backs that made it such a clean leg of the trip. I repeatedly caught myself smiling and noticed that my jaw ached because of it. I'd burst out laughing for no reason at all, and it occurred to me over and over again that, wow, happiness is the natural state for human beings, and perhaps all sentient beings, or at least mammals, and how sad it was that so many people on Earth continued to suffer so much and were somehow being kept from this natural state.

Todd and I went long periods of time without saying a word. I'd look over and see that knowing grin, and we'd nod about everything going so well. The slosh of the boat through the water was all the dialogue we needed. Pali was enjoying her own doggie, Sea Change, barking at whales, dolphins, birds, or for no reason at all, just as I would burst out laughing.

Before we knew it, we found ourselves avoiding cruise ships, meaning we were getting close to Cabo San Lucas, which is kind of a zoo for mooring a private vessel. We knew this and weaved our way through all that traffic. We turned inland around the tip of the peninsula, sailing a few more hours east before taking down the sails and motoring into the harbor at San Jose del Cabo, aka Old Cabo. It was a much more peaceful place to dock, in more ways than one, and undoubtedly more authentic to Mexican culture. We took a slip at Marina Puerto Los Cabos and intended to stay for a few days, have some fun in Los Cabos, and make sure we were ready for the rest of the sail down the coast before heading out again.

We got in the late afternoon after not seeing any real civilization, even remotely similar to the first world, in several weeks. In fact, it had been pretty much since we left Baja Norte that we had experienced anything like the United States. Cabo was a place I made some trips to throughout my life. The last trip down there was right after law school for a bachelor's party for my good law school buddy, Steve Helms. He married his college sweetheart, Charissa. It was a storybook romance, and the bachelor party was pure hedonism. It was probably the last time I had fun in my life before this journey. It was Steve's last hurrah, and in his drunken stupor, he was trying to sleep with anything remotely female. Some of his victims capitulated if they were also drunk or desperate, or he gave them enough *dinero*.

Steve and Charissa had a fairytale wedding where I was a groomsman. At that point, I had started at Owen and Owen and was so serious that I was even in the office before the wedding and didn't stay late because I was so exhausted from work. Steve and Charissa followed with a couple of kids and a nice home in suburbia. It turned out Steve's last hurrah in Cabo really wasn't his last. He couldn't keep his pants on as a young lawyer, and that led Charissa to drink. This all led to a caustic, viperous divorce.

Todd and I looked at one another with warm smiles once we got off the boat and sat down for a couple of mini-Coronas and fish tacos with lime all around. It was so stunning, and we felt so fulfilled and accomplished having made it to Cabo. We were giddy with excitement, like we were kids again. I had a strong Déjà vu of the time Todd and I were kids in Hawaii, and Dad told us he would get us surf lessons. We had great plans for all we wanted to do and even grabbed some cheesy fliers from a hotel of all the tourist traps.

We decided to go for a deep-sea dive and booked it right then and there for early the next morning. The boat taking us for the dive was within walking distance from where we were docked, so we got up groggily the next morning and did our best to focus on an all-morning lecture on SCUBA safety and technique. I had never gone deep-sea diving before. Todd had been with some buddies off Catalina once before. Once we got through the basic instructions in strained English with other families from *Bumfuck* somewhere in the Midwest, we went down with the instructor and did a few exercises.

Then, I was told to hold my nose and fall backward over the ledge of the boat. I did so, and there was an immediate feeling of peace once I got in the water and started breathing again. We took one of the instructors aside, and I gave him a hundred-dollar bill to take us down deeper and get us certified. We went down about 75 feet, and it was spectacular with all the species of fish, tigerfish, blowfish, mysterious stingrays, and happy turtles. I was down there in a daze, and a turtle swam by, smiling at me with the face of Buddha.

Exercising the *3PTs,* the Buddha Fields Techniques, I felt a certain calmness, accepted the situation, and took responsibility for my actions. I was still excited as we planned to travel down to Punta Mita, the Yucatán, through Central America and the Panama Canal. Life was blissful.

From San Jose del Cabo, we sailed South along the tip of Baja and found fun waves and good times at Shipwrecks, 9 Palms, and La Fortuna. Then the winds took us up out of the wave zone and into the Golfo de Mexico—the Sea of Cortez made famous by John Steinbeck. The region was spectacular. The vibe was positive, and there was so much upbeat energy. The water was azure with white sand beaches and abundant sea life.

Some of the passing clouds took the shape of Steinbeck's handsome face, and he described it better than I in *The Log of the Sea of Cortez*:

> *And we wondered why so much of the Gulf was familiar to us, why this town had a "home" feeling. We had never seen a town which even looked like La Paz, and yet coming to it was like returning rather than visiting. Some quality there is in the whole Gulf that trips a trigger of recognition so that in fantastic and exotic scenery one finds oneself nodding and saying inwardly, "Yes, I know." And on the shore the wild doves mourn in the evening and then there comes a pang, some kind of emotional jar, and a longing. And if one followed his whispering impulse he would walk away slowly into the thorny brush following the call of the doves. Trying to remember the Gulf is like trying to re-create a dream. This is by no means a sentimental thing, it has little to do with beauty or even conscious liking. But the Gulf does draw one, and we have talked to rich men who own boats, who can go where they will. Regularly they find themselves sucked into the Gulf. And since we have returned, there is always in the backs of our minds the positive drive to go back again. If it were lush and rich, one could understand the pull, but it is fierce and hostile and sullen. The stone*

> *mountains pile up to the sky and there is little fresh water. But we know we must go back if we live, and we don't know why.*[5]

We had scuba tanks on the boat and went for dives and free-dived with snorkels. We saw incredible species of fish, remarkable with brilliant colors and shapes. Snorkeling among the abundant sea life on a lazy afternoon in the warm, clear tropical water was my happy place: I felt free, alive, and at peace. We were insatiably searching for a mystic, secret spot that only breaks on certain swells. We found a sand point that had been discussed among some local surfers, and we were told that it was only accessible by boat and that it might be ideal in these conditions to break perfectly.

Also, we were told that it was only accessible by boat, listened carefully to some vague instructions, and were assured that *You'll know it when you find it.* Fortunately, we found the spot, and it was reeling perfect right-hander, chest-to-head-high waves down the line. Under the right conditions, the wave, which jacked up at the point, was a good half-mile long against a backdrop of beautiful, lush vegetation, including mature palm trees and white sand beaches, a true tropical paradise. The waves were perfect, not a drop of water out of place: turn up the face, make a turn, drop down the line on and on and on.

[5] John Steinbeck and Edward F. Ricketts, The Log from the Sea of Cortez (New York: Viking Press, 1951). This excerpt is taken from the narrative portion of the book, which is a portion of an earlier work, Sea of Cortez: A Leisurely Journal of Travel and Research. Copyright belongs to the respective authors and/or their estates.

CHAPTER 24

Shredding with the Buddha

Todd and I were blissfully trading waves one after the other at this *secret spot,* only to end up on the beach, walk a long way back, and catch another one. I felt in my peak mental and physical condition with indefatigable energy. After about an hour and a half of us blissfully surfing alone, a man appeared from out of nowhere. I don't know how he got there since there was no boat, nor did I see him paddle out. He didn't say one word. However, he surfed more gracefully than anything I had ever seen in my life—poetry in the ocean.

There was no verbal communication, yet there was an unspoken understanding: a wholesome, surreal, and magical mood overcame me. We spoke an ocean language of surf and style. It was a *body language*. As I paddled back out after a good ride, he caught a perfect little wave and sat on his board in a perfect meditative position: eyes closed, knees crossed. Sitting in a yoga pose, he had flawless trim and then disappeared into the abyss of a perfect, windswept barrel. Then reappeared, holding that pose.

The image was surreal, like a holograph framed in the sacred colors of the Shakra. He came, he surfed, he conquered, and then, just as magically, he disappeared. My brain didn't trust my eyes, so I asked Todd if he took pictures, as he often would paddle back to the boat to allow me a solo surf. Yet, in the pictures of the session, there was only a blur where the Buddha was surfing. I guess he doesn't like to be photographed. At that point, I knew the Buddha was the solution to my pain and suffering and existed there to give me a guiding hand.

We knew the next journey would be more arduous down through Central America, and we needed to stock provisions. We bought or bartered wonderful food from villages and caught plenty of fish—even invited some people aboard for cruises to fish, snorkel, or enjoy a beautiful sunset. This time up on the Sea of Cortez was really the most playful time on our journey.

We had to sail back to the new harbor right before the East Cape at Cabo San Lucas for provisions and a little bit of civilization before our long southbound journey—which was by design. We hadn't checked our email or messages for days to remove ourselves as much as possible from civilization because that is the effect the Sea of Cortez has.

There were a few important emails from friends. I had directed all work emails to my secretary or another partner, not wanting anything to do with automatic replies. I noticed one from our mother, who rarely contacted us—let alone by email. I also noticed she tried to call my cell phone. I opened the email, and it read as follows—sent to both Todd and me:

> Boys, your father had a heart attack. He is in the hospital, and we need you to come home immediately. Please respond and let me know that you received this message. These may be the last few days of his life.
>
> Love, Mom.

Leisure turned to frenzied haste—textbook "Buzz Kill." We emailed Mom that we were coming home as fast as possible. Both of us focused on packing up and getting back home as fast as possible. With remarkable diligence, we had all of our plans in place to store the boat and arrange for transportation back to LAX. We docked the boat in Cabo and handsomely paid a reputable company to pay the slip fees and take care of her.

We promised we would be back. We took the first flight home, in an exhausted, perfunctory state, anticipating seeing Mom and Dad in a new light. We settled back at Todd's place to regroup, showered, and changed into fresh clothes. It felt weird to be back so hastily when we anticipated the great adventure was just about to unfold. We called Mom and went to visit Dad in the hospital. I asked Todd to go with me, but he wasn't ready to see Dad yet.

I got the information from Mom and went to the intensive care unit to visit Dad. I walked into the hospital slowly in anticipation of seeing my strong father in an entirely different light. I got to the section he was staying in after finding it in the maze of people scurrying frantically around and so many rooms in the big hospital. The nurse pulled back the curtain in the unit where he was resting, and there was Dad, immobilized in a hospital bed with tubes going every which way. He could barely open his eyes; although he did so, he saw me, and he could muster a smile. Mom was there by his side. We sat for about half an hour, and she talked to me about his condition. Apparently, he was at work, and his secretary went into the office and saw him on the floor. The ambulance rushed to get him and took him straight to the hospital. They weren't sure if it was a heart attack or what had happened. Fortunately, it was just a stroke, not a heart attack, but still serious at his age.

After a while, I asked Mom to leave so I could be alone with Dad. When she left, I had tears in my eyes, seeing him in such a debilitating condition. I squeezed his hand with both of mine. He could barely talk and kept drifting in and out of slumber. I looked him in the eyes when he managed to keep them open and told him that he would get better and that we needed him in our lives. He looked at me and was able to mouth the words that I fully understood: "I love you, son." My heart melted in tenderness. Tears flowed from my eyes, and Dad also shed a tear.

My intuition was that this interaction was needed for his future after this lifetime. It was a beautiful moment, and I'd cherish it forever. I felt lightning in his being and mine. I visited Dad every day in the hospital, and I felt very close to him. Finally, a week later, he was able to go home but was told to take it easy. We were all relieved and elated.

Back home after the abrupt, unexpected interruption to our adventure, I was feeling the effects of the Sea Change. I felt like I had a future again and was destined to live as I wanted, as I entered this new chapter. I would be upbeat and inspire others around whom I had shied away before. I wanted to join our parents at their annual 4th of July celebration. There would be bittersweet memories from my former life at this formality—a mix of warmth, chilled by harsh criticism, ever-present family controversy, unbridled emotional unrest, and a hell of a lot of judgment.

I made a condition that if we continued the journey, we would go to the traditional 4th of July Barbecue dinner with Todd. It took me days of bugging, guilting, and cajoling until he finally capitulated and agreed to come. Todd mainly agreed just to shut me up and appease the family and his curiosity, as he had been pretty much estranged from any close contact. It had literally been years since Todd had spent time with our parents.

This time, I thought I could rise above: levitate like the Buddha, floating on a natural high and contentment. I showed up in nice jeans, boots, and a white embroidered shirt that I picked up in some remote beach boutique in Baja, and a great story along with that. My hair was naturally sun-tinted and longer than before. I was fit and smiled a lot more.

On the afternoon of the 4th of July, we arrived together as a gesture of our rediscovered Brotherly Love, a newfound friendship, and as moral support, knowing that we would be the targets of passive insults. We'd have to endure the same boring stories and gloating from people whom we did not consider genuine or kind.

These days, Todd has kept his arm's length from the folks.

However, it seemed that Dad was back to his old self. Or even worse, he was particularly tense, and we noticed his unusually quick and calculated mind drifting for the first time. His behavior was so unpredictable and ornery that I wondered and worried if he had early-onset dementia. Even Mom was getting annoyed at him. He sat outside talking to his friends and drinking a beer as if nothing had happened. Our Dad was still seething from the embarrassment and mess that I had created for him. He seemed to exploit any opportunity to mention it in front of others while looking sternly at me. I just smiled thinly and tried to calm my mind amid this onslaught of insults. Dad could barely hide his contempt and disappointment at how I *turned out.*

Dad quipped some particularly stinging remark as to how the year had been good, except for the cost to the firm of the incident with me. I tried so hard just to zone out on the words, but they found their mark and were hurtful. I felt internally numb and forgot exactly what was said—just that it was mean-spirited and unnecessary.

I regrouped and tried to shrug it off by changing the subject to the exciting Stanford Cardinals football team, who had assembled a great squad, particularly their offense. I tried so hard to relate to Dad. Of course, Dad only remarked that USC did not fare so well and that now Stanford had a superior sports program, and it was clearly academically the top school in California, if not the United States.

He mentioned how they only took the best and the brightest. Boldly, I feebly attempted to imply that even his Dad wouldn't get into law school according to today's standards. That caused another distinctly disapproving glare from dear old Dad.

Instead of the much-anticipated joy, I told myself and reminded Todd that we would experience, I felt empty inside, lost, upset, and even more alone than ever before. We both left shortly after dessert. Todd had just been quiet and polite, managing to sidestep the sharp criticism and other mal-intended remarks that were just like water off a duck's back. Todd was cool and handled any situation gracefully. We feigned affection for the family and friends with hugs and kisses. We bugged out early, claiming exhaustion from our travels. Although we had come back weeks earlier, there was truth to that—we were still tired. Or maybe we were emotionally exhausted from being around the family, which was the same old. We had evolved, and they hadn't.

We drove home and found peace, solace, and understanding in our Brotherhood. At home, it was cold and quiet. I felt insignificant and small, the party storming me with regrets about my entire life. I even wondered why I wasted so much time and money on the trip. Being used to having my Dad, colleagues, and a huge support staff, I worried about practicing law all alone.

I felt somewhat embarrassed, even with my own brother. However, I could pour my heart out endlessly, and he'd listen authentically to my worldly woes. Yet, he rarely complained. I mean, never... Nor did he chastise me. He never mentioned when I got stuck on the reef on a low tide in Mexico—now a past memory from those amazing days when we were exploring the unknown—to us, at least. Scoring perfect waves in perfect conditions with almost no one around in bona fide *secret spots,* we were exploiting along our journey.

From the natural world, I was back in the world, confronted by so many first-world challenges and questions. Will I make a shit-ton of money or just get by? As a lawyer, unless you're completely inept to the point of comatose, you should make a good living. A decent lawyer can make a hell of a lot of dough, and a great lawyer can kill it financially if they are motivated in the right direction.

"Do good work," I kept telling myself. "Help others." I'd hurt enough people and took away what was rightfully theirs by creative lawyering fueled by a shit ton of cash.

Some of the bottom feeders can live by ripping people off, even if they're too daft to realize it themselves. Bookworms, feeling that they are doing the world a favor with the benefit of their brain but really providing nothing helpful to their clients in return, don't contribute to society. I knew I could produce results, and that's what counts. I always maintained my confidence as a lawyer, even if I became complacent in the last round of my life, which I promised myself would change going forward.

I opened up again to Todd and shared my deepest and darkest secrets. I felt almost tearful about my constantly dumping on him, yet he took it like a rock—the rock in my life. We parted and gave one another a true brotherly embrace. It was this overwhelming feeling that came over me. I had never experienced true love. They say you love your brother. You should love your parents. I struggled with everything, but knew that at least my mother truly loved me. And I unquestionably loved her.

Male bonding is a form of love. A man and a woman, another. Mostly, my guy friends beamed with love when they talked about their children. Before my sailing adventure, I didn't care so much about kids in my previous life. On the trip, I appreciated the beauty and purity of children. They embraced joy and the moment with love and innocence. So many fond memories of this incredible circle of life for the kids we met and played with along the way. Our journey was timeless and carefree.

Every day was an adventure awaiting me with no real agenda. These children had virtually nothing, and some did not even have enough food to sustain themselves, yet they had a sense of contentment and wonderment glowing about them.

It was an infectious spirit, and I felt that being a daddy was my calling for the first time in my life. I remembered being a child, although that chapter in my life seemed to have been deleted from my brain while I was mired in pleadings, partnership meetings, client development (my weak point), billing (my high point), and making it to the next level—just trying to get ahead in the dog-eat-dog world I was so eager to join. I simply erased my childhood from my memory banks.

I often felt lonely, mostly on weekends, particularly as the end of a Sunday drew near. The monotony of the money-making method was wearing thin, but I was a high-paid drone. I now truly felt I wanted a child—hopefully, a boy to model after myself, but without all the many mistakes. I wanted to suffocate someone with love since I had been starved of it for most of my life.

It was also a great revelation that this was primarily my own doing. I could have released my anger, taken responsibility earlier, and had a family. That would have even fit in my role at Owen and Owen. At least someone had time to spend the money we all worked hard for. Many of my colleagues complained bitterly about their wives' spending habits. The spending often catered to their kids' inexhaustible search for the newest, *most fun*, and coolest game or gadget. Usually, this new item would soon be cast aside, with no child ever realizing that *money doesn't grow on trees*. These fathers often felt like they were running on a treadmill to support the lifestyle of their spoiled loved ones.

Boy, I was happy to sidestep that function where people paraded their families—all told to be on their best behavior. I tried to really avoid more questions about when I was going to settle down with a family, etc. First of all, nobody at Owen and Owen settled down, or the next train would run them over. Second, I wasn't too fond of the Stepford wives and bratty kids. That feeling about children changed when I realized they are pure, just a product of their environment. In the third world, kids were happy and innocent. They looked at you lovingly and with both compassion and fascination. I wanted to have a child of my own to mold a human being in the purest form and have fun doing it.

After the 4th of July Fiasco, it was a long and uncomfortable night. I was tossing and turning through the night. I was ruminating about where I was and where I'd come from—asking myself where I was going. I came to the stark realization that I had to forge my own destiny: planning my path in that direction. I was questioning myself, really thinking about my future, when I didn't have a Golden Parachute. Endless resources. Delegate everyone and bill for it.

I did, however, have a Golden Buddha watching my back.

I felt chilled to the bone from the weather changes into a slow winter and the night that didn't go as planned. I lived in fear and felt tremendous culture shock. People were distant, and I felt the world knew about my transgressions in my career path and some of my life choices. Many of them did indeed, but I magnified any opinions of others negatively.

My inner iPod was playing for this time after the abrupt end of the sailing trip, and the return to the World was *Should I Say or Should I Go* by the Clash. Because that was the battle in my brain: should I stay and throw myself back into the sharky cauldron of being a lawyer, or should I make the Sea Change permanent: go back to the boat, back to nature, back to the whales and the dolphins? "*If I say there will be trouble. And if I go there will be double. So, what I really want to know, is should I say or should I go?"*[6]

Private Practice

On a Monday morning in the late fall after a lonely, rainy weekend, I finally decided to jumpstart my life again after a long vacation. So, I set up shop by renting a nice office: a modest suite tastefully appointed with ocean images two blocks from the ocean near the Promenade in Santa Monica. It had a handful of other lawyers, including some struggling lawyers who fell off the proverbial pyramid. I made some friends but felt much the same as I did in the law firm, except nobody told me what to do, but I also didn't have a steady paycheck for that luxury.

The first disappointment was losing VitaPet, an overnight success selling purportedly healthy but over-priced dog food primarily to lonely old women with too much money. Their pet was the most significant figure in their life, and I was hoping VitaPet would be a significant part of my new practice. I brought in the client to Owen and Owen twelve years before. It was a great coup when a small, environmentally conscious, and natural pet product run by a few acquaintances became a multi-million-dollar annual revenue giant. The client's relationship was a boon for the firm. Being somewhat antisocial and arrogant, I wasn't a great rainmaker, but I was the company go-to man for this client and jumped on the phone listening to their long-winded issues while doing something else and billing for it, only to fob it off on an associate, forcing the client to repeat everything and creating a perpetual billing machine for the firm. Not being that outgoing, I could romance this nascent company with great potential and stagger the retainer, so they paid less upfront but more over time if they agreed to stay with the firm. There

[6] "Should I Stay or Should I Go," The Clash, (Combat Rock), 1982. These lines are excerpted from the song; all rights to the original composition and recording are reserved by the artists and distributors.

was an upside to the company doing well, strategically thought out, and probably above-board ethically. Still, when they took off successfully, it certainly warmed up the firm's fairly substantial annual income.

Under the canons of ethics, I was duty-bound to let clients know about any *significant developments* in their matters. Indeed, I was obliged to inform them of changes in their legal representation now that I was leaving the firm. The firm could do nothing about it. I mentioned to the dear client that I should consider coming with me when I hung up a shingle, which I intended to do once I got settled in.

VitaPet would be my Golden Goose—but it laid a rotten egg. I planned to undercut VitaPet's guaranteed monthly retainer from my former firm. That was $20,000 a month. To sweeten the deal, I requested only a $15,000 monthly retainer. However, that would not include any additional work that was not covered under the retainer. The retainer encompassed thirty hours a month at $500 for basic Human Resources advice, contracts, and minor business disputes, but not any major deals such as real estate acquisitions, major leases, or litigation. Fortunately, there was always additional work to generate more fees in addition to the guaranteed retainer. Now, I would do all the work myself. I used to be able to delegate it to associates and bill heavily for my time. However, I lost my *Gravy Train* from VitaPet, my former best client, which I was sure I would get and was counting on. It was another heavy blow to reality.

I figured that I would dedicate about one day a week to VitaPet, and I'd be all set. The fixed monthly retainer would cover my office and personal overhead. Anything else from VitaPet or other clients who strolled through my door was a windfall—found money. I had remotely romanced my buddy VitaPet Chairman Jared Stroller throughout the sailing journey. I thought we were friends, and Jared, as the founder/majority shareholder and COO, truly made all the decisions. I knew that from countless quarterly executive board meetings recapping the monthly board's minutes meetings. I believed that Jared made the decisions, and I stopped regularly going years ago. It was easier to send an associate and just bill for it. So, VitaPet seemed like a sure thing. I was comfortable looking forward to that security.

However, my arch-nemesis, Mr. Horowitz, nipped that in the bud. They invited Jared, along with his VP and CFO, to lunch, using the opportunity to sway Jared away from jumping ship from the firm to my budding law firm. They convinced him to remain a *loyal client* to Owen and Owen, not only because of the significant resources *The Firm* had. Mr. Horowitz also reportedly, at least I learned through the grapevine, politely warned Jared to steer clear of Dale's *poor judgment* and inappropriate behavior.

I anxiously called Jared one morning, thinking that this mega client would seal the deal. However, I grew anxious after I hadn't heard back from Jared for over a week. That worried me because Jared usually returned his calls reasonably soon, even though he was paying me for every need at that time. So, I emailed Jared, and after a couple of days, he replied with a terse and conciliatory but friendly email indicating that the board decided to stay with Owen & Owen. However, they wished me all the success in the world and would be sure to recommend me to any other businesses and executives looking for an attorney.

That trust I always felt with Jared was gone, and I guess I had bilked him for so long; I was pretty insincere when I was on my high horse, so it's just karma.

I was counting on this income stream from VitaPet. I wanted to return to a comfort zone in the first world. After it became clear to me that I had lost the client, I was fearful and angry. I felt again stunned by this cold world to which I'd returned. I reconsidered my decision to come home and start practicing law again. Indeed, I was kicking myself for not continuing the journey. Also, I felt blindsided by my rival Horowitz, who most likely defamed me. I imagined that Horowitz swayed the client by trash-talking me in as professional a tone as he could muster. He was always critical and constantly competing with me over the years. Certainly, Horowitz was unafraid to cross the line for the almighty dollar.

Should I Stay Or Should I Go, again now echoed loudly in my brain, but also Steinbeck's words: *One who was born by the ocean or has associated with it cannot ever be quite content away from it for very long.*

I had never seriously considered getting a tattoo because I thought they were gauche, but if I did, that quote from Steinbeck would have been it.

I longed for those lovely days on the ocean and regretted not continuing to sail my life away. I thought I could have stayed adrift, as Todd and I would often fantasize about spending our lives at sea. Given the circumstances, I could have done that. However, the truth was that when I was on the boat, there were so many times, like a hot, windless day at sea or anchored off some perfect point with no surf, when I experienced *ennui* and sank into a deep depression from sheer boredom and homesickness. Sometimes, while traveling, I wish I were at home, living in complacency and comfortably numb to the beautiful natural, fabulous worldly wonders out there, which I, more often than not when traveling, cherished.

Think of Captain Willard in *Apocalypse Now*: *When I was here, I wanted to be there; when I was there, all I could think of was getting back into the jungle.*

Exactly like that.

After getting the brush off from Jared, I wanted to be back in the jungle. After reading the email, I sat stunned and dumbfounded in my stale office and added up all my fixed expenses, including rent, for a grand total of $12,700. That's what I would need to make ends meet for the beginning of December. There were other bills out there, so I decided to defer in anticipation of hearty paydays from VitaPet. I had no income whatsoever and calculated how quickly my cushy nest egg would evaporate over time. The truth is, I could survive my life with security in a modest condominium and a tight budget or undoubtedly have a great life aboard our yacht—or another one I contemplated buying when I was so into sailing at times on our magical trip. I could envision the sea as my forever home. Although sometimes, during a particularly rough patch, the thought sickened me.

But there are many different kinds of storms.

Sitting cross-legged on a couch pillow, I meditated and thought of The Three Priceless Techniques, telling the receptionist to hold all calls and then lock the door. It was the only thing I could do to wipe away the grief and pain. Meditating while in the ocean or at a port had been easy, but it wasn't as easy in the real world. It occurred to me that I was my own boss and could live by my own rules. I decided to go off to some tropical paradise to surf my brains out to regroup before delving into the law again; this time, only answering to myself.

On the sailing trip that was fading into a distant memory, I had more perspective, particularly at sea. From the vantage point of looking in from the outside and dealing with the self-actualized life on the journey, I looked forward to returning from the trip as a new man. I had to regroup and try to clear the constant chatter from my mind. I visualized myself as calm, cool, and collected as the Buddha himself slowly came down. I felt a sense of quietude and serenity overcome me. I started feeling the warmth and freedom of the ocean air in my mind's eye, recalling that wonderful surf day in that unknown bay in Mexico where I was at one with the Buddha. Feeling better, slowly, I knew I'd gain perspective to pick up the pieces and move on.

My grief persisted over several days. I mustered the courage to reach out to my high school college girlfriend Laurie, who was seeking much-needed comfort from my old flame. She seemed so excited about going out on a Tuesday night in mid-September when she could finally break free. When we met at a popular beach restaurant, she looked ravishing as she sauntered into the restaurant. The meeting place was an old, familiar family steak house called *Crowley's* because I thought revisiting a special place where we spent so much of our younger years might inspire old hormonal memories. It was a local watering hole where we went out after high school graduation in a bygone era.

She had become *vegan,* which made ordering from the carnivorous menu uncomfortable—like going to an oyster bar with a Rabbi. I wanted steak but ordered fish while she had a beet salad.

It had been years since we saw each other, and I was nervous yet extremely hopeful that we would pick up where we left off once again and be a Golden Couple. I was overwhelmed by old emotions and her glow from an earthy, natural lifestyle, actively preserving her younger self. She didn't look much different, maybe a few wrinkles here and there on her face, and she had not quite as tight a body as she once had, but she was close. She followed an authentic skin, diet, and fitness routine rigidly. I embraced her passionately and was surprised that she gently kept her distance as I moved in to kiss her.

"Damn it," I thought I'd already blown it and should have been more reserved. We sat down at a table I cherry-picked to recreate a romantic situation. Eventually, things eased up, and we flowed into a comfort zone. Casually, I reached for her hand later, which she grasped onto, then quickly let go. We reminisced and laughed about old times. There was a moment when I felt nostalgic and genuinely thought that I reclaimed her as mine and fate would take its course. Lo and behold, I was besotted again.

(Vibe song here? *Taxi*, by Harry Chapin: *She was gonna be an actress, and I was gonna learn to fly*.)

We parted sooner than I wanted or anticipated, as she claimed an early morning meeting. After a nice, long, delicious dinner and a lovely stroll down memory lane, we kissed on the lips. I thought for sure that my new and improved, hip, fit, soulful self would effortlessly win her over again, and it was a *shoe-in.* Particularly in view of our close history and, more recently, very loving cyber-interchanges as we flirted together along my journey. I included her in my adventurous sea change and would regale her with my exciting encounters and insights that I had learned along the way.

The next day, I received an encouraging email from her thanking me for the dinner, emphasizing how nice it was to reconnect. That email seemed more formal and distant than the playful, suggestive messages she would send me on my trip. I immediately asked about seeing her on Saturday for the new movie we talked about at dinner, making tentative plans to see it on our *next date,* as I suggested. Days went by, and then she responded that the holidays were so tough and that she hadn't done any gift shopping for Christmas. Maybe we could see each other then? I took this as a hopeful gesture that she was interested, but swamped and just wanted to do the dance and allow everything to fall into place and seal our fate together.

For two weeks, I sent her messages in various forms, such as emails and texts, and I finally called her. I was crushed when she didn't return any messages. Finally, on Christmas Eve, I sent her a bold email, expressed my tremendous affection, and said that we were meant to be together. Days later, she got back to me, saying that she cared for me but was on and off with "Roger," whom she'd never previously mentioned. She gave me the death stroke: she loved me as a friend, but wasn't ready for a relationship. I suddenly felt like that arrogant prick whom she broke up with years ago. I was uneasy, angry, and sad. I was the asshole again.

The *friend zone* was not friendly—words I'd heard throughout my life, but I thought this was destined to be different. I just thought it would be smooth as silk, and we'd pick up where we left off. I was devastated and kind of pissed at the same time. I thought she was like every other woman in LA and that Roger was convenient. I tried to fish for information on him through social media. I looked him up, compared myself to him, and was overcome with emotion at how I had lost out again to some lucky kook named "Roger." This blow from left field truly crushed and blindsided me. I felt a huge emotional void and again turned to Todd with my heart thumping loudly on my sleeve.

Surprisingly, Todd just said, "What did you expect? That you two lovebirds would just ride into the sunset and live happily ever after?" I felt that even Todd didn't care and that I couldn't even turn to my brother and my rock, and I felt wholly rejected by humanity.

Again, I went on another health cleanse and lived a simple life devoid of distractions. My focus was on setting up my new office. I ate cleanly, almost vegan—inspired by Laurie—and did not consume too much food. I focused on a healthy lifestyle of yoga, paddling on a SUP that I bought used from my neighbor. As a surfer, I was initially reluctant to try standup paddling because surfers looked down on standup paddlers as kooks. But then I tried it and found what excellent exercise it is and another way to get into the ocean regardless of waves and tides. Soon enough, I had a SUPiphany: I was hooked and couldn't get enough. I would paddle for exercise and catch great waves. It was like learning to surf all over again.

Also, I became sober. Upon returning from our sailing trip, I went for a physical examination by my regular physician of many years, Dr. Peter Martin. Dr. Martin was an affable fellow and a straight shooter.

He was very impressed that my blood pressure was much lower, and I checked out physically much healthier than at the last examination some two or three years before. Dr. Martin did note elevated liver enzymes. He asked if I drank alcohol. I responded that I had "a few drinks a week."

He suggested I stop for a while and get re-examined. That was all it took for me to write off booze. I never looked back because it never tasted all that great to me, and I realized most of the stupid and dangerous behavior came out of people when they drank too much. I was "California Sober," continuing to take a hit of pot from time to time, but then I just stopped because it seemed everyone else was on the wagon. It was also losing its effects after I was smoking it frequently and freely among surfers and sailors along our journey.

I took hikes in the beautiful, scenic local trails with a good amount of rain for greener pastures, which I hadn't done since junior high school and mostly on field trips. I meditated deeply every morning and night and thought of The Second Priceless Technique. Gradually, I saw everything with an effervescent, rainbow-like aura of *Buddha Fields.* Everywhere I looked, I saw grace and beauty. I forced myself into every situation with those rosy-colored Buddha glasses. When I first returned from my sailing journey, it was challenging to continue sitting practice. I missed the serene melodic sounds of the ocean—the Blue Mind, some people call it. I was usually undistracted when on the boat, particularly out at sea. It was just so easy to meditate to such a deep level that I felt as if I were levitating.

I felt sorry for myself and continued to be deeply sensitive, which was different from the emotionally void feelings and stoic behavior I had before this enlightenment. I could not understand why I was so upset about my hopes of a romantic fantasy with Laurie being dashed. After all, she was my first, and I believed we were destined for true, lasting love. I thought for sure we'd rekindle that old flame.

Todd still wasn't helpful, listening to me bemoan my lost love on every occasion we talked or got together. Finally, one day, when we snuck out for some herbal tea, he looked me straight in the eyes and said: "If you replace expectations with appreciation, your life will change instantly." I thought about this poignant, Buddha-like philosophy and practiced appreciating all I had. I embraced incredible gratitude for all the gifts that had been bestowed on me. Despite money going out and not coming in, I felt confident about my burgeoning solo law practice.

I then started a website and actively solicited business, mostly from other lawyers who were too lazy or incapable of following through on their own cases. I referred them out to try and make an easy buck. Mostly, I romanced successful, established lawyers with case standards so high I could take on their table scraps. I met with several, was finally offered, and took on a case from an older plaintiff's lawyer I'd known for many years through my family and from crossing paths during law practice. Slowly, cases and clients trickled in.

Also, I snail-mailed out fancy announcements of my new venture to all my contacts. Surprisingly, this more senior attorney, Jerry Engbloom, called me when I mentioned in the announcements that I would be willing to associate on existing cases over litigation or trial. Truth be told, I had three cases to verdict as first chair earlier in my career and defended them. These were sure, winnable cases. They were frivolous lawsuits where the plaintiff could not sustain their burden of proof.

Our firm's practice was primarily to bill as much as humanly possible while working up files and settle just before trial any case that we'd potentially lose and even some we thought we'd win. We could have tried to settle when we got the case, but that wasn't our *business model.* The firm had an insatiable thirst for billable hours. So, we endeavored to thwart or ignore opposing counsel's overtures toward resolution and continued to *churn* the matter, creating a lot of meaningless work and sharing our client's indignation that such a *frivolous case* could be filed against them, regardless of the merits. We could also win the proverbial war of attrition by overworking and overspending the opponent. As defense lawyers, we didn't have the burden of proof. Juries have become cynical and conservative, and I have not lost a trial even though the cases I defended were so frivolous. It was incredulous to think that any attorney would see them through to a verdict for whatever ridiculous reason.

I boldly impressed upon people that I'd never lost a trial. It might have been teetering on the brink of being unethical, but what the hell… it was true. I met with Jerry for lunch to discuss the case, and then, later, the prospective client was in Jerry's office. The name of the prospect was Lindsey Graham. Not the Honorable Senator from South Carolina, but a woman who filed a salacious harassment case against her employer.

I was excited about the prospect of trying a righteous case. As Jerry labored hard for years in contentious litigation, he was sufficiently prepared, thinking that the case would settle for high six figures. He could warm up his bank account enough to retire and live out the rest of his life moderately with his wife and close-knit family, including two children and five grandchildren.

Norm Bailey founded Bailey and Associates, a blue-blood accounting firm grossing about $5 million annually. Old man Bailey was indeed a good old boy. At seventy-three years old, he never learned political correctness and relentlessly tried to lure Lindsey into his bed. He made scandalous remarks to poor Lindsey, a single mother with an eight-year-old son, Lucas. She was just scraping by as Norm's administrative assistant, earning $17 an hour after four years of working tirelessly with no benefits or bonuses.

Numerous times, Norm threatened Lindsey with termination if she didn't comply with his lewd advances. Finally, only Lindsey and Norm were working late after a particularly frustrating Friday. Norm often demanded she work without paying overtime without, even as much as a thank you, so when the staff and everyone had left at about

6:30 p.m., Norm wasted no time summoning Lindsey into his office. He proceeded to undress and assault her sexually. She managed to extricate herself with her clothes half undone since Norm sloppily grabbed at whatever buttons and zippers he could. Fortunately, she took pictures and still had the clothing, which she didn't use or wash, showing small rips and tears. Lindsey went home feeling dejected and lost. She sobbed uncontrollably all weekend.

She needed this job for survival and thought she'd just gather her courage and continue to work to support herself and her young son Lucas, barely getting by every month as she had no support. She was estranged from her son's father, whom she barely knew and certainly didn't have the willingness or means to pay child support. She was abused as a child by her Dad, and her Mom was an alcoholic who passed away when she was thirteen. Her Dad, who was real trailer trash, only came around when he needed something.

When Lindsey arrived promptly at work by 8:30 a.m. one Monday morning, Tammy asked the officious office manager to come to her office. She was handed a termination notice signed by good old Norm himself, basically saying that they didn't need her anymore. She was paid for the pay period but offered no explanation, severance, or appreciation for her years of undying loyalty to Bailey and Associates.

Lindsey found Jerry on the Internet as he touted himself as an aggressive and outstanding Wrongful Termination Attorney. Jerry thought his ship had finally come in. He figured this could lead to a quick and lucrative settlement, given Norm's heinous behavior. However, when Jerry's settlement demand letters were ignored, he filed a lawsuit, thinking that Bailey and Associates would finally roll over and settle. On the contrary, they denied everything and hired the law firm Logan, Walters, and Emery, who came out swinging. To his credit, Jerry hung in there and did what was expected, figuring a big payday would come. He deposed Bailey and did the minimum and a reasonably competent workup.

After discovery was completed with a trial date looming two months away, the offer Jerry had been waiting for was finally communicated. To Jerry's shock and extreme chagrin, it was a mere $20,000, which was an insult. The defense didn't believe Jerry had the wherewithal or ability to try the case. Lindsey would get scared into submission of a low settlement because they would *rake her over the coals*. Alternatively, they threatened her (never in writing) with the time-honored: "You'll never work in this town again." Of course, comments like this were egregiously illegal, although it mattered not in the least bit to them. The defense had no regard for doing the right thing and was hell-bent on making Lindsey's life more miserable than it already was.

With nowhere to turn, Jerry asked me to take the case over. He'd help with 50% of future costs, and we'd split the fees 50/50 in case of settlement or verdict. I was happy because the discovery had been completed as well, as our experts had been deposed. The defense experts were set for the following week. We arranged to meet with Lindsey that Friday morning at 10ish. I wanted to see how she'd appeal to a jury and if I was committed to this case before I decided to take it to trial. Given the disparity of the demand and low-ball offer in the litigation, it appeared to be heading to trial. She was available since she was still not employed, so she had nothing else going on.

Lindsey showed up, without calling, forty-five minutes late. She was haggard and dressed in old jeans and a tiny blouse. I was annoyed, but we all regrouped and sat in Jerry's office. When she explained that her kid was sick and she had no help, had to find someone to watch over him and scrape together gas money, and her phone was turned off, I was no longer irritated. Instead, I felt deep sympathy for her, and I could see that she was a rather attractive, slim brunette with kind eyes but radiating a world of hurt.

When she was seventeen years old, she left high school and took the proficiency test in the middle of her junior year. She had no interest in school and was impregnated by an older twenty-year-old *boyfriend* whom she only dated for four months. He worked stocking at a warehouse when he could hold onto a job; she seemed relatively bright and articulate. She had a very simple and genuine way about her. Her speech was somewhat rough, albeit sincere. She thanked Jerry and me profusely for our help and apologized for any inconvenience she might have caused by her being late.

There was a sense of yearning and desperation in her voice as she asked us if we thought her case was winnable. Jerry slapped me on the back, saying I was a great trial lawyer from a big firm who knew all their dirty tricks. He told her he thought the case was a sure winner. I tempered his enthusiasm and told him there were never any guarantees, but she had a strong chance of winning, although our justice system was imperfect. Judges or juries could be fickle and unpredictable when moral decisions are left up to humanity in this day and age.

The defense attorney, Michael Perkins, was smug, belittled the case, and deprecated the client when I introduced myself. He was surprised when I handed him an association of counsel pleading and told him I'd be trying the case. He chuckled and indicated I'd be essentially wasting my time fighting a losing battle.

The next day, I effectively deposed the notorious Dr. Moriarity, a known psychologist defense whore commanding $750 an hour (with a two-hour minimum) for his testimony. I hadn't taken or even attended a deposition in many moons, yet auto gear and my lawyerly instincts kicked in. He couldn't seem to recall, let alone calculate, the outrageous amount the defendant had paid him in their feeble attempt to buy justice. He opined that the client was essentially delusional and set up her poor Norm, whom he portrayed as the victim, after the deposition. Perkins continued his chortling and said I was making a *terrible decision* if I were to try this case. He laughed outright after the firm had done an extensive background check on me and told me this case was a loser. He had some connections at my former firm, saying this case was not the way to resurrect my career since I'd clearly fallen off the proverbial pyramid.

Perkins' defense was to fight a war of attrition by boldly intimidating his opponents, such as Jerry. They had a seemingly bottomless pit of money and resources fueled by sadistic anger. He lacked any sympathy and appeared to be devoid of any emotions. I came to a striking revelation that he was me a year ago. A money machine who only wanted to win at all costs. *Unpersonable* and lacking in character. It reminded me of my old self… I vowed that I could overcome this and justice would prevail. I was angry and emboldened, ready to go to the mat rather than running away.

The song that propelled me through all of this was *Rise*, by Public Image Ltd. "*ANGER IS AN ENERGY*!!!!" These people pissed me off because of how they were trying to buffalo Lindsey and belittle me, and how, in the words of John Wayne in *True Grit* and Val Kilmer in *Tombstone*: "They remind me of me." I was determined to defeat me—the old me—in the shape of him and them.

I took their economist's deposition the following week, and he was somewhat dry, just another bean counter whose name slipped my mind. His opinion was vague and based on variables. The trial was now six weeks away. I had a lot of time to prepare, which meant reading all the lengthy depositions that Perkins and his associates had taken and voluminous discovery, mostly just endless, meaningless paper-pushing by the defense.

Suddenly, I felt different. I felt alone. All of these years, I never really developed any real friendships or deep connections with anyone other than Todd, who was now working hard after our long, fantastic adventure together.

CHAPTER 25

Escape to Fiji

I was chasing the carrot on a stick, trying to get ahead. Interpersonal contacts surrounded my life, and our interactions were shallow. Even our parents needed someone. I felt so intensely lost and lonely. This was a different sadness than when my life fell apart with Bianca and the firm. This time, it was not that emptiness of disrepair; I felt hope deep in my heart.

I was angling for more business the following week, but my efforts fell flat. Something wasn't working as I was out of sorts and longed for adventure. I missed the road, the tropics, and the carefree lifestyle. I was trying to apply my *Buddha Vision*; however, my glasses were foggy.

And again, it was painful to think that the approximately $20,000 in expenses I was paying every month would last me half a year out at sea. Longer. Cash flow needs are low when your only major expenses are gas and docking fees and whatever provisions you can buy from a fishing village, and you are living off the sea.

I got that wanderlust again and needed to do something about it. It became wildly apparent that applying The Three Priceless Techniques on my travels was far easier. I was pensive and wanted that sweet sense of freedom and exploration that was so satisfying to my soul. The South Pacific beckoned me—like Bali Hai in the *South Pacific*. Other than our annual childhood Hawaiian vacations, I hadn't ever been there. I had a month without any real obligation before I had to come back for trial. I reminded myself that several weeks back, I promised myself to get lost in another tropical paradise, and the press of business seemed to overcome my desire for a great escape.

So, again, I went into power mode, prioritizing getting out of dodge into the white sand and azure waters of the South Pacific. I rationalized that going to the gym and warming up with light weights was akin to applying The Three Priceless Techniques on vacation. And it was time for a warmup! Without hesitation, I bought a one-way ticket to Fiji. I packed my bags, knowing I could rent surfboards wherever the waves flourished, and three days later, I landed in Nadi. I took a room at the Sheraton to figure out where to go next. I didn't want one of those planned surf vacations. So, I rolled the dice, jumped on a plane, and reacted to whatever unfolded when I arrived.

It was a night flight, and very uncomfortable in coach class on Fijian Airways. Previously, I'd always flown Business Class. Candidly, I did miss that perk on this particular flight.

I arrived bleary-eyed in the morning and said, "Well, how did I get here?" as the moving melody of *How Did I Get Here by Talking Heads* played in my head. I couldn't just continue to escape life so my problems and intense loneliness would fade away. The most beautiful tropical island in the world and the love it evoked seemed to evade me somehow, although I was in the thick of it. After a bizarre taxi ride speeding along the bucolic countryside, numbly watching local Fijians tend to their livestock and till their fields, I arrived at the Marriott Hotel. Physically and emotionally exhausted, I slept most of the day and talked to no one. That night, I lay awake alone and lonely in bed, thinking life had passed me by and I needed to do some good in the world and develop genuine friendships. I didn't tell but a few that I was going away. Of course, I asked Todd to come, knowing he couldn't afford it financially or timewise and secretly just wanting to be alone with my thoughts—"On the road like," Jack Kerouac. Or maybe Jack London. Mark Twain.

I couldn't sleep from jet lag and so much angst about my direction and purpose in the world. I sat on the veranda gazing at the incredible stars—brighter than I'd ever seen—listening to the sea's ebb and flow lapping gently against the shore and looking at the luminescent moon and abundant stars. I was wide awake yet lost in deep thought.

I thought about how my whole life had been somewhat of an existential crisis. I continued to ask myself: "What did it all mean, and why was there so much injustice in the world?"

For the first time in my life, I empathized deeply with the senseless suffering of children and animals who were helpless. I felt ashamed that I was born with a silver spoon in my mouth, yet I hadn't made one iota of positive contribution to humanity.

I heard that commitment was needed to change. I was done with the suffering and committed to applying and perfecting The Three Priceless Techniques for my and all beings' benefit! I suspected the Buddha was watching over me from his *Buddha Balcony* and was proud of me. I would make a difference, starting with Lindsey's righteous case.

For years, I had taken so much from so many. Now, it was time to give back.

Particularly, thoughts kept ruminating in my mind about a case I defended at trial where I knew my client, a wealthy banker, had committed fraud. I hid evidence in discovery from a deserving plaintiff. Sam Bowers was a decent, hardworking, kind, elderly family man. He took out a second mortgage on his home, which he owned outright, and raised his kids there. My client, First World Bank, was a predatory lender that preyed on others' economic misfortune. Sam got caught up in the whole mortgage crisis. He made timely payments to the banker, but the banker changed his address, which was essentially a ploy to claim he didn't receive payments.

The lender calculated that nobody would read the entire email and the weekly newsletters. In the letters, the fine print sandwiched in the middle of the document stated there was a change of address to which payment needed to be made. I advised my client not to make a prudent economic decision to settle as it might open the floodgates to further litigation. I knew that Sam and his simple, country-bumpkin lawyer didn't have the wherewithal to properly try the case, all the while knowing this was a ruse for the banker/predatory lender to foreclose upon unsuspecting prey of poor, unsophisticated homeowners.

Sam's low-rent lawyer was pathetic and barely put up a defense. The Judge didn't care or pay attention. He took the least resistant path, so we won a directed verdict after putting on our case. Young and brash, I was fine with that, even though Sam lost everything, including his home, financial nest egg, *Mom and Pop* hardware store, livelihood, and, mostly, dignity. Worse yet, I never thought twice about it before that night. A feeling of tremendous guilt haunted me from deep in the past. It felt like a ton of bricks had crashed on my head, and my body was Mike Tyson's punching dummy.

I was guilt-ridden and felt terrible that I ruined a good man's life. I never thought twice about it before; I just gloated about my victory. I didn't give a rat's ass about Sam, his family, or anything else for that matter. Overcoming my emotions and self-pity for the man I had become, I had to reach out to Sam.

I had heard from one of my attorney buddies who was an alcoholic that Alcoholics Anonymous calls this Step 9 of 13: *Make direct amends to such people wherever possible, except when to do so would injure them or others*.

I was able to find old emails and wrote him the following email:

> Dear Sam,
>
> I'm not sure if you remember me. I was an attorney for the First World Bank. We had a case years ago and beat you in the trial. The judge stated that the foreclosure of your property was proper. I now realize that I did a terrible thing. The lender did not give you adequate notice. I have been guilt-ridden about that and wanted to reach out to you and ask you for your forgiveness. I am so sorry for what I did. I have changed my life, and I want to right this wrong if there's anything I can ever do for you.
>
> Regretfully,
>
> Dale Owen

A few days later, I received the following reply from Sam.

> Dale, thank you for your kind message. I was furious at you and the bank, but God has given me forgiveness. People at the church helped out, and we're back on our feet. How could I ever forget you? You were a bulldog lawyer; I know you were just doing your job. May God bless you and your family.
>
> Sam

It was a cathartic moment. Relieved that Sam had forgiven me, I promised myself only to pursue honorable and honest cases and do the right thing. I sent Sam another heartfelt email expressing just that. His response, which concluded our conversation, was *God Bless.*

The wind was howling on our little island in Fiji (Alexa says there are 148 islands in Fiji; I thought there were at least twice that many). Taking advantage of the resort, the guests were mostly honeymooners or families. Feeling I didn't fit in, I needed to find somewhere to go where I could be alone with my thoughts and challenge myself in the powerful Fijian waves. I knew the Marriott would be a short stay.

However, before I left, I rented a Hobie Cat at the resort and had a blast feeling the wind in my sails again—soloing on a mean keel. It was pure joy until I capsized. Unable to right the Cat—since every time I tried to lift the pontoon, I got blown away—they had to rescue me, much to my embarrassment. I was a good mile out when a very dark man with very white teeth came out full speed on a motorboat. Together, we lifted the catamaran and towed her back to shore.

Shortly thereafter, I found myself on a puddle jumper marveling at a handful of the many islands that comprise Fiji (about ⅔ are inhabited). On the internet, I found a quaint Eco Lodge on the island of Bega (*ben-gah*), just south of Suva. Their vacancy was down, and I was able to book a *Bure.*

The buzzing of the puddle jumper went away, but not the annoying chatter in my mind. The Fijians who greeted me with a warm *Bula* were instantly calming as these large, South Pacific islanders radiated warmth and what Hawaiians call *aloha.* They lived in the moment, even though they had no material wealth, and life was hard for them. They were pure and kind and embraced beauty, music, and laughter.

On the plane ride from LA, I began to read a Buddhist book and learned that *kleshas*, in Buddhism, are mental states that cloud the mind and manifest in unwholesome actions. They included states of mind such as anxiety, fear, anger, jealousy, desire, and depression. For a moment, I thought I saw my picture in the book as these states of being accurately described my life as an attorney. Reading about *Kleshas* gave me more resolve. Reading was something I rediscovered on my sailing journey.

While back in California, after I set up my office and put my lawyer hat back on, old habits die hard. I had fallen into the same rut I had when I was in the firm. There was so much anxiety and discontent. Also, my healthy lifestyle had fallen by the wayside. I had lost almost twenty-five pounds and was at my leanest, but I gained about fifteen back. I felt bloated and sluggish. I wasn't exercising as much, although I would go back home for a short surf. I wasn't doing yoga, routinely meditating, or certainly not eating as well as I did on the trip. I thought that I had lost so much weight and was healthy that I could cheat a little bit by having some sugar-processed foods here and there. Unfortunately, I again began eating such bad food regularly and rarely ate healthily as we did on our trip, making all kinds of excuses and falling into the same routine.

A good night's sleep swept away my *mindwebs.* Perspective sharpened. As the brain fog began to lift, a feeling of peace and warmth overcame me. People kept to themselves and let me do the same, yet they were friendly and authentic.

There was no social climbing or condescending attitudes. Every night, a gentle rain enveloped the jungle surrounding my *bure*. It felt so calm as it was pattering on my thatched roof. There were times in my life when the last place I wanted to be was alone with my thoughts. Now, I was at peace, alone with my thoughts again. And I began to feel healthy and took yoga to better my time in the surf. I had nowhere to go and had to go all day to get there.

Before my time with Todd on the boat, I had rejected spirituality. I avoided any connection to "New Age," shunning it as mumbo jumbo—a waste of time for the weak and the meek. Todd often spoke about famous philosophers and spiritual guides during our journey. The only decoration in the small bathroom on our boat was a framed, tattered sheet with the words for *Desiderata* pinned next to the wall of the head to give us something to ponder as we peed. In a wise poem written centuries ago by St. Francis de Assisi, *Desiderata* spoke to me, in particular, one sentence. "Many fears are borne from loneliness and fatigue."

At some point in my sea change, I had the epiphany that my adult life was plagued with loneliness and fatigue. Money was not buying me happiness, without any real purpose or goal to enjoy it.

DESIDERATA

.....

GO PLACIDLY AMID THE NOISE AND THE HASTE,
and remember what peace there may be in silence.
As far as possible, without surrender, be on good terms with all persons. Speak your truth quietly and clearly; and listen to others, even to the dull and the ignorant; they too have their story. Avoid loud and aggressive persons; they are vexatious to the spirit. If you compare yourself with others, you may become vain or bitter, for always there will be greater and lesser persons than yourself. Enjoy your achievements as well as your plans. Keep interested in your own career, however humble; it is a real possession in the changing fortunes of time. Exercise caution in your business affairs, for the world is full of trickery. But let this not blind you to what virtue there is; many persons strive for high ideals, and everywhere life is full of heroism. Be yourself. Especially do not feign affection. Neither be cynical about love, for in the face of all aridity and disenchantment, it is as perennial as the grass. Take kindly the counsel of the years, gracefully surrendering the things of youth. Nurture strength of spirit to shield you in sudden misfortune. But do not distress yourself with dark imaginings. Many fears are born of fatigue and loneliness. Beyond a wholesome discipline, be gentle with yourself. You are a child of the universe no less than the trees and the stars; you have a right to be here. And whether or not it is clear to you, no doubt the universe is unfolding as it should. Therefore be at peace with God, whatever you conceive Him to be. And whatever your labors and aspirations, in the noisy confusion of life, keep peace in your soul. With all its sham, drudgery, and broken dreams, it is still a beautiful world.

Be cheerful. Strive to be happy.

Max Ehrmann

Time was my own; I didn't have to be anywhere or answer to anyone. I was eating fresh eggs, fruit, and fish, and instead of coffee or soda, I drank herbal tea or pure juice and coconut water, detoxifying from the bad habits I had resorted to during my time back in *the world.* Near my *bure*, there was a fantastic yoga studio. It was built in the eco-forest with open, high ceilings and a commanding view of a Banyan tree in front of the deck, which I would fixate on while doing yoga poses, particularly the tree pose. Over time, I began to slow down and breathe again—feeling lithe, strong, and vibrant—energized by the ocean and nature and living what Costa Rican *ticas* call *pura vida.*

There was a gorgeous yoga teacher named Sonia. She spoke perfect English with a slight accent. I couldn't figure out where she was from and didn't have the moxie to ask. I was in my own world and didn't think she would want to be part of it. (Doing the *wo-math,* Sonia was

Audrey Hepburn times Zoey Deschanel.) What some call *pale* but the English prized as *fair,* her unblemished skin was the clearest, softest, most beautiful I had ever seen—a testament to clean, clear-minded living. Her limber, petite frame was complemented by thick, shoulder-length auburn hair, which sparkled like the aurora borealis in the sun. Yet it was her eyes... She had captivating eyes that shone brighter than the stars in the moonlight. If eyes are the window to the soul, I wanted to slide them open and slip in.

One day, I was doing my Savasana, and she came up with eucalyptus oil and rubbed it on my shoulders. Her touch was soft and gentle. Understandably, engaging in daily yoga, her body was athletically toned and natural. She was about 5’3”, and her soft voice had so much beauty and clarity, which enunciated every syllable in a sing-song with impeccable diction. I detected her accent and thought it was European, although it wasn’t clear where it was from. Nor could I tell her age. She had a body like a twenty-year-old but spoke wisely beyond her years.

Sonia intrigued me, and I would learn so much from her vignettes of wisdom during our guided meditation and classes. She was strong but supple, and her step had a bounce. She had an amazing vitality; her presence stimulated every fiber of my being. No longer would I have to drag myself to yoga or do it out of obligation. I couldn’t *wait* to go to yoga. She talked about breathing in slowly, yet her presence made me almost hyperventilate. I began to go to class to be around Sonia, but I felt my body changing, becoming more robust, more flexible, and clearing my mind.

It became a daily schedule of a solid half hour of my morning routine of sitting practice and journaling in silence, alone with my thoughts, eating pure food while surfing the powerful, often perfect Fijian waves. Sonia’s yoga hour became symbiotic and ingrained in my persona. Yoga would help my surfing and vice versa. I was transfixed by her powerful presence and perfect poses. I felt so smooth and solid, getting lost in the stillness and strength of her precise teachings. However, I never talked to Sonia. She seemed to have a wall around her heart and kept people at arm's length. She was not among the guests or staff; she appeared to be in her own world. Other than yoga, I rarely saw her. If we happened to run into each other, she would smile and gently say "Hello," yet she seemed unapproachable.

Tongue-tied, I never knew what to say to break the ice with Sonia. Finally, one day after class, I worked up the confidence to ask her about the Warrior 3 pose, which I was genuinely interested in. She lit up, and after the other students had cleared out, she bent and manipulated my arms and legs to do the pose correctly. Afterward, we hung out in the studio for about fifteen minutes, just talking. It felt natural for us to walk away from the studio together. So we did and continued our wonderful, comforting chat.

When I asked her how long she'd been practicing yoga, she said she started at twenty-two, meeting her master at a ripe young age and continuing to practice for twenty years. I was shocked to learn she was forty-four years old, as she looked ten to fifteen years younger, particularly with her porcelain skin that was so perfect. That flowed into her accent, and I learned she was from a small town in Germany near the Swiss border. She asked where I was from and what I was doing in Fiji. I gave her the Reader's Digest version of my history, emphasizing my recent trip and other places I had visited: Mexico, Central America, and the Caribbean. Although she had never been to North America, she had traveled throughout Europe, Asia, Africa, and Australia.

She was highly educated, having earned an advanced degree in Chemistry from École Polytechnique. She followed that with a successful career with Sturm und Drang as one of the principal chemists. After twenty years, she had retired with stock options and a pension, enough to allow her to travel the world. She was an intellectual in the physical and social sciences. Well-versed. Her French was flawless, and her English was perfect, with a slight, charming accent.

Captivated by tales of the sea, she listened intently to the details of my sailing trip with Todd because she was fascinated by sailing.

My internal mood music for Sonia was *Brandy* by Looking Glass: *Yeah, Brandy used to watch his eyes, when he told his sailor's story. She could feel the ocean fall and rise, and she saw its raging glory.*[7]

Sonia was indeed a fine girl, and I even got in trouble a couple of times when I called her Brandy—by mistake or jokingly.

"Who's *Brandy*!?" she was her initial nearly violet retort. My adroit attorney negotiation skills were also deployable in my personal life and got me out of this quagmire a couple of times…

[7] "Brandy (You're a Fine Girl)," Looking Glass, (Looking Glass), 1972. These line are excerpted from the song; all rights to the original composition and recording are reserved by the artists and distributors.

CHAPTER 26

Awakening

Something stirred profoundly in my heart. Yet, I also told myself that she was out of my league. Perhaps we could be friends—a goddess like that would never really be interested in me romantically. Our get-togethers became a regular daily event; we would talk and get to know one another. We would go have tea after yoga. Time just seemed to drift as her unbelievable beauty and charm captured me. We became so close, and we opened up to one another. It became so comfortable to be with her. She was like this angelic friend with whom I was besotted.

She was a friend with benefits. No, I mean the yoga was the benefit. Sonia opened my hips, heart, and mind at the same time.

Time gets funny out in the tropics, but I figured out I had been there for two weeks. I knew my time was limited in this romantic paradise with the object of my undying affection. I had to get back to reality within the next week to get to work and prepare for the trial. Theme music here, *Back to Life* by Soul II Soul:

Back to life, back to reality
Back to life, back to reality
Back to life, back to reality
Back to the here and now, yeah[8]

I was kicking myself for taking the case because I could've stayed longer. My yoga practice intensified as I became incredibly flexible, and so did my interest in Sonia.

She told me about a beautiful walk to the waterfall and asked me if I wanted to go the following day, saying she didn't want to go alone. It would require most of the day, and we needed to leave early to get back in time for her 4 p.m. yoga class. I jumped at the chance, trying not to appear too eager. I knew that the surf would be great the next day, and I was looking forward to it, but I was happy to forsake great waves and spend all day alone with Sonia in the rainforest. I was setting up for my next move. I had to tell her how I felt when I worked up the courage.

We got together that morning to load up a backpack with water, snacks, some fruit, and sandwiches. Slowly, we walked together away from the resort to the rainforest. I was elated as it was magical to be with her. She began to open up even more to me and feel more at ease since she was somewhat reserved and guarded at first. She was almost shy and kept to herself.

I learned eventually that she had married her first love, Thomas. She met him at eighteen, they married at twenty-one, and were divorced by the time she was twenty-eight. She was still apparently heartbroken. She said they drifted apart over time as he began drinking and could not maintain a job. Sonia always said Thomas was extraordinarily talented, creative, and idealistic. She always wanted to have children, but he

---

[8] " Back to Life (However Do You Want Me)," Soul II Soul featuring the Reggae Philharmonic Orchestra and Caron Wheeler, 1989. These lines are excerpted from the song; all rights to the original composition and recording are reserved by the artists and distributors.

never committed to it or tried to have kids with her. Also, Sonia wasn't sure that he could support her, let alone a family.

Thomas was a musician but could never make money from his passion. He could play many instruments, primarily the piano. However, he couldn't always pay the rent, and she joked that the instruments took up most of their flat. He would sit around all day playing music instead of working. She became resentful, and he retreated... Sonia said she tried hard to make it work, but left after giving him many chances. After that, she went on the road from one exotic place to another as a yoga teacher. She just wanted peace, security, and doing what she loved.

Indeed, once again, I found my paradise. This time, every fiber in my body was alive with the feeling of love. I felt again in good shape and ready to surf big waves. I ate purely organic food, and yoga was fabulous. I'd been surfing pretty much every day. It was nothing perfect, but a few fun shoulder/ head high-plus waves were getting my groove back. These waves were local gems that the boatmen knew like family.

I was always greeted with a friendly *Bula:* Fijian for *hello,* but with more behind their word. Polite, warm, peaceful, happy people, it was easy to see the Fijians as Buddha in applying Priceless Technique Number Three. They were gracious and appreciative, never taking anything for granted, including their simple possessions and lifestyle. Whenever there was an interchange with a Fijian, it was always followed with a beaming smile and "Vinaka," which means "thank you." Strangely, the strong, rugged, fearless Fijian warriors were the gentlest of all. They always wanted you to be happy and charm everyone with their air of confidence. And they knew how to have fun. They would take us out to the best breaks; some of them would even surf with us, but always encouraged us to take waves, never dropping in on anyone.

Whatever the Fijian word for *aloha* is, these guys had it.

Somewhere over the horizon, miles out to sea, there was a mystical surf break called "Frigates Pass." The name had come up throughout our Mexico sailing adventure. I recalled meeting another surfer/sailor somewhere in Mexico who said that Frigates was his favorite break, describing it with such excitement in his eyes about how fabulous and challenging it was in such a beautiful, remote place. It was about an hour-long boat ride through the famous Bega Lagoon from the resort to an open ocean reef.

With our stoked, strapped, affable young Kiwi ripper and surf guide, Nate, we strategized the optimal time to go. Based on the conditions, he selected a random Wednesday morning. We arose at the crack of dawn amid roosters chortling, packed provisions, and motored about an hour out to the break: pristine waters under a pristine sky out to a pristine reef, far, far, far out to sea.

When we got there, the wave was peeling perfectly: a perfect left spinning over a crystal clear, but very shallow and sharp staghorn coral reef.

I was the first to wax my board, jump in, and make the long paddle in the warm, azure water. Freaked out a bit by that paddle through deep water to the relative safety of the reef, my heart was pounding, and I wondered if that vibration might attract sharks. I sat wide of the break and watched it explode on the coral reef. I'm a regular foot, but I figured I could handle this left because it was so perfect. Riding a wave like this backside makes you look straight down on the reef, and I knew that failure could be costly as the sharp Fijian break is notoriously unforgiving. (If a visitor even *thinks* of touching that staghorn coral, they get staph. I was amazed by the Fijians walking over the reef in bare feet.) I waited for a few waves and paddled, but did not get any. Then, a couple of other people from the boat joined the lineup.

I was in a position on a wave that was so big I heard the water roaring as it approached like a freight train. I was scared out of my wits. All the surfers I got to know were mainly Aussies and another Californian. They hooted loudly, encouraging me to paddle hard. Feeling my heart in my throat, I put my head down and paddled with all my might. As I pushed my board's nose, angling its rail hard to the left, feeling the undulating water, the wave started to lift me like I was defying gravity.

I paddled once, then with two more solid strokes, and it felt so good. There was a slight hesitation in my mind as I was making the drop while grabbing the rail. Thinking now or never, I pushed myself up and somehow got to my feet, riding the wave backside. Finding my balance in the powerful surge of water, I made a scary but fabulous free fall and carved left up the wave's face, zipping down the line, climbing, and dropping. It was a thing of beauty. When I kicked out of a tubing wave at the end, I felt so incredible, hooting and feeling on top of the world. The stroke propelled me back out to the break, and my confidence was skyrocketing. That was one of the best days of waves I'd ever surfed, if not the best. I took some great waves and got a lot of sincere compliments from the guys.

Twenty miles out to sea, far from land but danger-close to that sketchy staghorn reef, I was scared, but the more waves I caught and made, the more my confidence grew. The go words in my brain were "drive," "stay alive," and "thrive." I did so as I powered through the breaks, continuing to take off on waves with confidence. Eventually, a boatload of friendly Aussies pulled up, and I bugged out of the lineup, feeling on top of the world. I was exhausted. After climbing up and collapsing on the boat, I drank some fresh coconut water and ate a mediocre sandwich that tasted like manna.

(You know that marketing expression "Only a surfer knows the feeling?" This is what they're talking about: surfed out, exhausted, hungry, healthy, strong = stoked!)

Back at the resort, I asked myself, "How could the day get better?" I was looking forward to Sonia's afternoon class… I showed up eagerly. When I got there a few minutes early to lay on the mat and stretch out, she looked at me with those big blue eyes and said: "Dale, I'm so glad you're here!" in her slightly accented, singsong voice. My yoga and confidence flowed! I was feeling good, but eager for it to be over so

I could just be with Sonia. I felt so powerful and practiced The Three Priceless Techniques of seeing myself as Buddha, the world as a *Buddha Field,* and all as Buddhas! I was so entrenched in the feeling, and I felt the Buddha's presence.

After class, Sonia waited patiently for me. I sat next to her, and our hips and knees touched. I was wearing shorts, and she was wearing a sexy little yoga outfit. I suggested that we go for a stand-up paddle. She was so intrigued and not well experienced, so I grabbed her a 10-foot board and grabbed myself a 9'6 paddleboard from the abundant quiver of great SUP for the guests. We launched off the beach and began our paddle into the sunset while everyone else enjoyed cocktail hour.

We were talking as we paddled next to one another into the clear tropical water and over the kaleidoscopic species of vibrant fish frolicking below. She told me of a gorgeous private beach on the island, suggesting we paddle there. We had a nice leisurely glide bathed in the blue sky, azure water, and so much color. Landing smoothly, I pulled up the boards onto the sand, and we started walking and talking. For the first time, I told her my story, and she listened patiently. She never really inquired much about me. However, when I began to open up, she listened intently, gazing deeply with eyes as blue as the Fijian sky and clear as the water over the reef.

We sat on the beach—the last two people on earth—and I unraveled my life. She listened intensely and with empathy to everything I had gone through. I owned up to the fact that I was the architect of my premature demise. Sonia was enthralled with tales of our recent sailing adventure, asking all kinds of questions about places she wanted to go. Of course, she provided encouragement for my new vision and interpersonal growth.

An hour passed, and after a long silence, I gently took her hand and told her I had strong feelings for her. It was hard to get out because I was so intimidated by her beauty and grace. She looked at me, and then we collapsed into each other's arms on the beach, kissing passionately.

Sonia and I became emotionally and physically connected on a profound level. Except for my dawn patrol sessions, we were inseparable. We held hands while kissing and embracing tightly every waking moment we were together, excluding my surf sessions. Then we would spend nonwaking moments and would sleep together. She would sneak in my *bure* after dark. It was beyond blissful engaging in pillow talk, making love, having her body next to mine, and waking up together every magical morning.

At some point, I had to break the news that I would be leaving in three days. I thought about giving it all up and living in the Fijian paradise with her. However, it just wasn't in the cards at the time. I didn't want to leave Sonia, but I couldn't abandon Lindsey—she needed me, too, but in a different way.

The last few days, we both felt the pain of our impending separation. After my morning surf escapes, I was eager to be back with her. She was very private and didn't want other people to see us together, so we would go on walking, paddling, or snorkeling excursions to various places close yet far enough away on the island. We ate together, not with the others; we would grab our delicious, healthy fish from the daily catch, locally grown chicken, fresh fruit, and rendezvous in my *bure* or on the beach away from the crowd.

The last night we spent together, that night in my bed, was both painful and beautiful. Things had progressed relatively slowly with her.

The next day, she got on the surfboard with me. All the way out to Frigates Pass, she sat next to me, her leg touching mine, while holding my hand. My surf buddies I'd befriended on the trip were shocked because this was a spectral woman who kept to herself. Besides her classes, which she taught elegantly and gracefully, nobody saw her around the eco-resort. For Sonia, I wanted to show off my surfing prowess by slaying the last of the dragons. The waves came up and were the biggest and heaviest waves I had encountered on that trip.

Those same well-traveled swells that hit California with such surprising force were something wilder and more powerful out in the middle of the Pacific. While snorkeling on a break from surfing, I swam to the edge of the reef, a sheer cliff that dropped straight down into the black. Swells traveling through deep water trip abruptly over the reef and roar forward with all their power. Thrilling and frightening. A challenge to ride.

After catching my breath, observing, and getting into the lineup with a few other guys I had gotten to know, I confronted my fear and paddled with commitment. As the waves began lifting me, I jumped to my feet. I slowed down the line by dragging my left arm in the face of the wave to get as deep in the barrel as I could. I caught a few waves and felt delightful all over. Having such an adrenaline rush while being deeply in love was a great combination.

And having the love of my life watching from the boat was even better.

I knew that I needed Sonia in my life. However, I felt a sense of loss knowing that I was leaving and feeling that this unbelievable experience was just another fleeting romance, and we'd probably never see one another again. I wasn't sure if this was real or just a dreamy moment of bliss. I felt love in my heart, yet I wasn't sure if she genuinely felt the same way after I was burned so severely by Bianca. However, I knew Bianca was just a fantasy, and Sonia was the real deal, practical geographical considerations aside.

Sonia even rode an hour to the airport with me, and it was a tearful separation when I had to board the plane. She opened up and told me at the last moment that she had been suffering a broken heart ever since her divorce and was searching for escape, trying to find solace by traveling and doing yoga. I reciprocated, telling her I thought the same way. We are committed to exploring our extraordinary union further.

So, we agreed to see one another as soon as possible. I fell into my window seat on the puddle jumper to the main airport in Nadi with a heavy heart. I was in a euphoric state yet feeling lost without her on the flight home to LAX, but I couldn't sleep just thinking about our fairytale romance, asking myself if we were for real. The theme song/ mood music here is a lovely, sad, tropical tune by Leon Russell, *Back to the Island*:

Now the day is gone and I sit alone and think of you, girl
What can I do without you in my life?
I guess that our guessing game just had to end that way
The hardest one to lose of all the games we played

But the time is past for living in a dream world
Lying to myself can't make that scene
Of wondering if you love me or just making a fool of me
Well I hope you understand I just had to go back to the island[9]

[9] "Back to the Island," Leon Russel, (Will O' the Wisp, Side Two), 1975. These lines are excerpted from the song; all rights to the original composition and recording are reserved by the artists and distributors.

CHAPTER 27

Dale's Return

I returned tan, fit, healthy, happy, recharged, and ready for work mode—ready for battle—raring to go forward with the trial. I was excited with a new lease on life, feeling content about my trip: The pure food, surfing, yoga, relaxation, breathing, and meditation were wonderful to reenergize my soul. I felt grounded. More importantly, I was in love and felt light and happy, yet uncertain if this was just a fleeting island dream or the real deal.

I felt ready to add more weight to the deployment of The Three Priceless Techniques. My *Buddha Suit* fit better, and I felt like a luminous litigator: empowered, seeing myself as a Buddha and my world as a *Buddha Field.*

Reality slowly set in as I showed up at the Final Status Conference (FSC) with the judge before trial. Wanting His Honor to be his most enlightened self, I visualized him as a sagacious Buddha sitting on a throne. As I applied this Third Priceless Technique, it seemed that his rate of speech slowed, as did his breathing, and he seemed less in automatic mode and more present.

We started picking a jury—Voir Dire—after reviewing pretrial motions with the judge. Things were getting down to the wire. The judge does his job by questioning the jury, and then the plaintiff's jury goes first, as we have the burden of proof. I wanted to pick the most enlightened jury possible, the ones who could correctly see the merits of our case. I started seeing the potential jurors as a collection of Buddhas.

Seeing them as a group was easy. There were a few individuals; however, I couldn't hold the visual. Their demeanor and outward appearance challenged my *Buddha Vision*, and my *Buddha Suit* started fraying a little when I realized I hadn't perfected this Technique. Upon this realization, my suit started unraveling even more. With my thoughts and emotions not under control, it was clear that I was caught in a Samsaric world and not a Buddha Field.

The judge kind of *split the baby* on the rulings, but I was satisfied that we would get a fair trial, especially since the courtroom felt clear. I started reflecting on The Second Priceless Technique and how our environment affects us. If a courtroom's normal stress and aggressive, *warlike* energy could truly be transformed into a *Buddha Field,* this might do wonders for my cases. My attorney mind kicked into gear, and this sounded far-fetched, but I was already noticing something different in the room, so more analysis was needed.

We were gearing up and getting everything ready, which is a monumental undertaking for a jury trial. The ever-present butterflies were fluttering as I'd never felt before. Truthfully, the earlier trials were all overprepared by eager associates with nothing better to do than manipulate who would overbill hours the clients would pay under the pressure of a trial.

Truthfully, there was much less pressure in my cushy job at Owen and Owen. My pride and a client's loyalty were all I had to worry about previously. Win, lose, or draw, we got paid. If I won, I took all the glorious limelight; if I lost, I'd blame someone else. This was my day for great inner reflection, as this model was no longer *Buddha-worthy.* I was always annoyed that politicians on TV never fix a problem, but just blame their predecessors. This consciousness in our world was prevalent, and I suddenly wanted to emulate Gandhi and *Be the change.*

Preparation of the case and state of mind are key. I had brought copies of all the depositions on the trip and thoroughly read through them and other documents in the case. I spent more time agonizing and meditating, visualizing a big verdict with a Giant Buddha blessing the *Buddha Field* courtroom with all in attendance as Buddhas. It was magnificent! I felt enlightened, as prepared as I could be and had to leave our fate in the hands of the jury.

The Honorable Judge John Schneider was our trial judge. He was previously a Deputy District Attorney who had a good reputation as fair-minded and ruling on the evidence. Now that he was transformed into the Honorable *Buddha Schneider*, I felt even more confident. In other words, he would really allow us to try your case without getting caught up in evidentiary objections or mundane details.

That would mean His Honor, at his discretion, would allow evidence to be presented to the jury unless it were clearly inadmissible, and I felt that would help us. Every trial lawyer knows it's a huge advantage to have the judge on your side. He had a robust, traditional demeanor and ran his courtroom with an efficient, no-nonsense dignity.

When he called our case for the trial calendar, I buttoned my imaginary *Buddha Suit Jacket* and confidently declared: "Dale Owen, ready for trial." My opponent did the same. I calculated an honest assessment of my deployment of The Third Priceless Technique, and I could only see his *Buddha Suit*, maybe up to his knees. Instead of getting down on myself and tattering my own *Buddha Suit*, I chalked it up to my just learning the Technique, and it would take more time to perfect it.

As I used my mind positively and kept my emotions moving toward a more exalted state, I felt my *Buddha Suit* growing in stature! It felt like a pocket square emerged with more defined pinstripes and sheen. It was an *Ermenegildo Zegna-Buddha Suit.*

We went into the Judge's Chamber to discuss the case further and review some last-minute pretrial rulings. Walking into his stodgy, overly filled-with-books and lifeless wooden furniture environment, I immediately felt the difference between the now *Buddha Fielded* courtroom and his *Samsaric* office. Judge Schneider asked if we could settle the matter. I looked at my opponent, and he shrugged, saying it didn't hurt to try. I think I got his *Buddha Suit* up to his bottom suit button as things started to flow.

I believe I even noticed the dark gray energy around his head was lightening up. Wait! Did I just see energy around his head?? I did! In my excitement, I had to maintain my composure and follow what was also happening in the physical world. Since Judge Schneider would be our trial judge, it was the best practice for him not to engage in settlement discussions, so he sent us out to a mandatory settlement conference with a volunteer attorney.

There was more posturing and bravado from the defense. While he was doing this peacock thing, I think I even gained another button on his *Buddha Suit.* What was cool about this application and maintaining my *Buddha Suit* and *Buddha Field* is that I wasn't getting caught in the normal whirlwind of intensity. I was detached, at peace, and mentally and emotionally clear. The whole environment seemed to slow down. When I played tennis, I heard of great tennis players who said the ball slowed down for them, which was now happening to me!

They offered $75,000. We would've settled for $150,000, although I told them we needed $250,000 to resolve the case. I was awaiting a counteroffer, and there were none. We knew they would probably pay $100,000—expenses already incurred were already over $30,000, so settling at such a low number wasn't worth it. However, we would have considered it if they had offered $100,00. The opposing counsel's *Buddha Suit* transformation was complete, and he was even glowing now. As such, we were unable to settle. While I saw him as a Buddha, the defense maintained his smugness. The judge said we would return the following day and start picking a jury. We went home.

I called and texted Sonia, but she didn't get back to me that day. As the day faded into night, I felt lost, thinking Sonia was over me yet maintaining hope that she would still be captivated by the magic we created together. My confidence was waning. The next morning, I woke up to good news: I received a long text from Sonia again, pouring her heart out, declaring that we shared common ground, chemistry, and compatibility, and she wanted to give us a try. Priceless Technique Number One was slipping away from me with these mind-clouding *kleshas*. Her tugging at my heartstrings was also pulling at the seams of my *Buddha Suit.* Both were starting to fray.

I felt good and did yoga again; I then went to a little cafe for breakfast before the court to study the *Voir Dire* questions I had prepared to ask the jury and trial notes. I had slept soundly and appeared in court refreshed and feeling good that morning. The judge told us he had to finish another trial and come back tomorrow to start ours.

The following day, when the trial would commence by starting jury selection, I got up early. To calm my nerves, I applied the First and Second Priceless Techniques. My heart rate instantly slowed, as did the racing thoughts in my head. My body even took a deeper breath of its own accord. To me, the most accessible place to experience a *Buddha Field* was on my board. The surf was good; even though I had to be ready at 10 a.m., I thought I'd paddle out for a few waves to clear my head and stimulate my overworked, stressed body and brain.

Court is a place where you need and want a clear mind, and spending a little time in the ocean is the best way to clear the mental palate.

We commenced with *Voir Dire*, which means to *Say the truth* in French. The goal was to determine if the prospective jurors were appropriate to sit on the jury and render an unbiased opinion based on the evidence they would hear. The more intelligent jurors who wanted to get out expressed some kind of prejudice. A couple of wobblers ultimately said they could be fair jurors. I was worried about many of them who stated they thought jury verdicts were too high. They rambled on about how people regularly exploited our system of justice for money, but these people did not know the facts.

Instead of playing a song in my head, I recounted how many times I had to explain to a client, *Liebeck vs. McDonald's* (1994), where a woman sued after being scalded by a cup of McDonald's coffee. I had to correct the client that the woman was rewarded millions for medical expenses and punitive damages. When, in truth, the trial judge reduced punitive damages to $640,000, and the parties settled confidentially before it was appealed.

I carried that sentiment into the jury selection. I never felt so comfortable asking jurors questions, remembering their names, easily looking at them in the eyes while moving around, and taking a genuine interest in their responses. The Three Priceless Techniques were working like a charm! Before, jurors were a means to an end to be manipulated and confused by the evidence, which is an advantage to the defense. Now, I saw them as people with hearts and souls I need to explore to see if they could be a fair and impartial jury that I could persuade with the evidence that there was a severe injustice that needed to be righted by them.

I allowed them to talk to determine if they had any prejudices. A few of the jurors were challenged for cause, and the judge dismissed them for various issues. I exercised four of my peremptory challenges, and the defense exercised all six of theirs. Finally, we selected a jury of twelve with two alternates.

I could only hope they would see through the smokescreen of the defense's case and do the right thing. We went through the motions of selecting a jury that didn't whine about the trial and explained why they couldn't uphold their civic duty. It always amazed me why people would say things such as, "My employer doesn't pay for jury duty" or "My kid has a doctor's appointment." In such cases, the judge wouldn't care and would not excuse the prospective juror from service.

Even with the jury panels' more legitimate excuses, he interrogated them in open court or chambers. I thought Judge Schneider would be very insightful as I understood he was a good prosecutor before being appointed to the bench. Nothing was getting past him. He allowed some of the real sob stories from prospective jurors on the jury. He did not want to appear too harsh, and I respected him.

The judge didn't exclude much evidence, as the defense screamed bloody murder about every shred of proof that would help our case. The defense was attempting to keep all our evidence away from the jury. They tried to excuse things like the fact that Lindsey had a son or how much money she was making at the job and these fundamental things. They used the old Evidence 352 Code, which was more prejudicial than probative, arguing that it was "Damaging to their case."

Of course, the judge saw right through it, suggesting/accusing that they were worried that some of our credible evidence might persuade the jury to see the truth. Judge Schneider basically let all our important documents in to show the jury, while the defense lawyer was increasingly becoming more uptight.

CHAPTER 28

The Trial

Deploying all of The Three Priceless Techniques, seeing Judge Schneider as a Buddha, the opposition and the jury as Buddhas, and all in the *Buddha Field* courtroom as Buddhas, we made our opening statements and put on the defendant under Evidence Code 776 as a hostile witness. He looked nervous; he was a big man with gray hair wearing a blue suit. He was well-coached by his lawyer, but we scored many points when I cross-examined him, and he became unraveled as he squirmed in the witness seat. His body language suggested he was not telling the truth, although I'm sure he had rehearsed his words many times.

"The burden of proof is on the plaintiff, Lindsey Graham. We will prove to you, ladies and gentlemen of the jury, that the defendant sexually harassed her, creating a hostile environment, ultimately resulting in her termination." I opened with this to the jury with great conviction. I tried to be *folksy,* Gerry Spence-like. Before, I didn't want to cozy up to the jury; I just wanted to see justice prevail.

Ultimately, after we empaneled the jury, which took an entire day, that was still efficient based on the clockwork precision of Judge Schneider's courtroom. Again, I was happy that we were moving forward and felt I could accept a fair jury after I was excused for peremptory challenges and the defense used all six of theirs.

I sat down after I made my opening statement. I thought it was compelling. The defense kept saying I had the burden of proof that "Lindsey threw herself in the arms of the defendant." Evidence will show that she is manipulative and set up her unsuspecting victim, who was a pillar in the community, raised four children, had seven grandchildren, and one more in the oven.

Counsel listed the defendant's charitable activities and dedication to his church. Lies, all of them, I thought to myself, the jury will see right through it. I reinforced my vision of the jurors as Buddhas. I was hoping that I was helping to enlighten them. Maybe it was my imagination, as it seemed there was a giant bubble shield around them. The opposing counsel's sophistry-laden argument seemed to bounce off the shield.

Judge Schneider, who was still commanding but acting more Buddha-like with a softer tone and air, told the plaintiff to proceed. "Plaintiff will call the defendant as a hostile witness under the Evidence Code 776," I announced with authority. I blindsided them right out of the gate. The defendant sluggishly stood up, composed himself, and took the stand. He was rotund, his face red and bloated. He was groomed and wearing an expensive, light-blue Brooks Brothers pin-striped, blue suit. Mine was a thin gray Armani, as I'd recently bought two snazzy new suits from Nordstrom at their annual sale, and they were custom-tailored to fit and flatter my surf-and-yoga-toned, *Buddha-enlightened* physical form.

As suspected, the defendant admitted to having an affair with Lindsey. He said she came on strong. He reluctantly succumbed to this young temptress when she threw herself at him, ripping her clothes off after they were out for a happy hour and had a few too many. The defendant said that Lindsey threatened to tell his wife if they didn't continue having sex and she continued to get raises, she'd go public with their salacious affair. Finally, he said he had to have her fired by the Human Resources department because she "Screwed up too often."

I cross-examined him with screenshots of some texts that Lindsey had saved. He replied, "I don't remember saying all of those incredibly descriptive sexually explicit things that I wanted to perform on Lindsey."

Norm Bailey further suggested that she could have created those text messages herself despite having subpoenaed her phone records. We attempted to obtain Bailey's phone records through discovery, but they played Artful Dodger, using every excuse in the book, ultimately claiming he had changed phone numbers, and it wasn't worth the fight since we had our own records. I made a big point of that and mentioned it several times during the cross—that they were deliberately trying to hide these records.

The defense fought hard to remove Lindsey's text messages from the evidence and away from the jury. Still, Judge Schneider, bless his Buddha's heart, unequivocally declared: "The text messages are admissible, and it is for the jury to decide if they are real or not."

On the stand, Norm feigned a soft, avuncular approach in a feeble effort to "kill 'em with kindness." However, Old Man Bailey was shaking in his boots, guilt-ridden, and fell apart during his testimony. I exploited this vulnerability to excoriate him on the stand.

The cross-examination went like this:

Q: "Isn't it true that you came on to her?

A: "No… She came on to me."

Q. "Isn't it a fact that Lindsey's clothes were ripped?"

A. "Uhhh, I dunno."

Q. "Isn't it true that you had sex with her?"

A. "Yes, but she wanted it."

While he was answering the questions, I remembered the Third Priceless Technique. I took a deep inhalation and saw him as some kind of *Buddha of Compassion.* I shifted my state of mind and tone and compassionately asked, "Why did you do it?"

Norm's eyes watered. He started balling like a toddler and all but confessed: "I had been so miserable in my life and marriage. Lindsey was so tempting and vulnerable—she made me feel like a king, and I couldn't help myself..."

After I completed his cross-examination, I thought we'd already won the trial. Assuming that the defense would come running after us with a check, I was shocked that there were no more settlement overtures after that fiasco by the defendant. Instead, we just had more paperwork from the defendants as they continued pulling every little trick in an attempt to slow down the forward progress.

It was time to put Lindsey on the stand. I gave her a $100 bill to go shopping. Overjoyed, she went to Ross' Dress for Less and came back looking appropriate and groomed. I told her to tone it down as she was attractive, and we didn't want her to appear like a seductress. She did an excellent job on the stand, looking at the jury with slow, well-rehearsed answers to the softballs I was throwing at her in my direct examination. At one point, she started to cry uncontrollably. I really thought the jury was sympathetic as they watched her intently, taking copious notes.

We took our lunch recess and continued her examination after we went over it again at lunch, telling her to slow down her responses and look at the jury. As a matter of scheduling, we took a couple of percipient witnesses, Lindsey's friends and neighbors, who all testified what a hard worker she was and how this upset her. They said she constantly struggled, and since she lost her job, she was on the brink of economic disaster. We broke for the day around 4:15 p.m., as the judge said he had to attend a judicial meeting.

We finished the day early at 3:30 p.m. since the Judge had a few matters he needed to attend to. After I went home for a turbo snooze, I worked till about 12:30 a.m. and awoke surprisingly refreshed, sleeping a few hours quite deeply, then getting up at the crack of dawn to surf. I got a few decent waves for maybe 45 minutes. I was hoping the Buddha would reappear, but he did not. I went back home, showered, jumped in my car, and arrived at the Courthouse a few minutes before 10 a.m.—arriving at the exact moment the officious clerk opened the doors. I took that as an auspicious sign that things would work out for me.

The following day, they put Lindsey on the stand for cross-examination. Admittedly, she'd forgotten some things, and she got flustered. Again, I tried seeing her as a strong Buddha; this time, it seemed to have little or no effect. The defense was browbeating her, but there was little I could do.

She seemed fragile and would stutter or forget her responses. I was just hoping the jury could see that they were beating her up and she was defenseless. They scored some points on impeachment matters that were not entirely on point, but still made her look not completely honest or at least not very bright. I think it was the latter. Overall, they didn't score too many points, and I thought we still had a good chance of winning the trial.

The defense put on their case in chief after finishing with Lindsey. Their experts didn't say anything I wasn't expecting because we took their depositions, and they tried to contradict our experts. They looked like hired guns, and their testimony was transparent. I thought things were going our way, and we were close to getting the case to the jury.

We then put Lindsey on the stand for direct examination. The Defense objected to almost every inquiry as being obstreperous and interrupting our flow while simultaneously trying to intimidate her. For one dramatic moment, I declared in open court: "Lindsey has nothing to hide from the jury," as I'd heard so many plaintiffs' attorneys say before. That used to always annoy me.

Despite all the obfuscations and demurrers, Lindsey told her story. I asked her if she was nervous when she took the stand, and she admitted she was. I imagined her to be a strong Buddha to give her strength. It became clearer to me that there were different types of Buddhas; some were QUITE STRONG and POWERFUL! It seemed to work as her testimony unfolded. She was able to talk about the experiences she went through and fear for her survival and her son—of whom she was the sole support—if she didn't capitulate to her boss's lascivious demands.

As the trial unfolded, it put our experts on the stand, but nothing earth-shattering came of it. Our expert opined that Lindsey had suffered economic damage in the $400,000 range, based on the fact that she didn't get another job for a long period of time. Our overeducated and overpaid psychologist astutely talked about how Bailey victimized Lindsey from his position of power and prestige by using *transference,* which is defined by healthline.com as "a phenomenon that occurs when people redirect emotions or feelings about one person to an entirely separate individual."

As expected, all the defendant's witnesses were current, long-time employees, and they reiterated the party line: Lindsey was bad news. She was insecure, thrived on male attention, and had provocatively solicited all the men at the firm for sex. Finally, the defense's last surprise witness was Lindsey's former boyfriend and her baby daddy, Henry "Hank" Wilcox. He was not on the witness list. We fought like hell to keep him out, but the defense produced an investigator who said he had just located him and was put on as an impeachment witness. Of course, that was absolute BS.

After a long argument at the sidebar, Judge Schneider excused the jury and wanted an offer of proof so the defense could put him on the stand. I cross-examined him, but, to my shock and chagrin, the Judge allowed him to testify.

He said he was on a *Short leash* after more arguments on the record in the Judge's Chamber. The defense bought and paid for Hank Wilcox, Lindsey's ex-husband. I had no compassion for him. He was verbally and physically abusive to Lindsey before, during, and after their marriage. He never cared about their son and used him as a pawn to control and intimidate Lindsey. Throughout the boy's life, he barely knew his father; maybe only once in a blue moon would Hank take his son out for a happy meal.

The sight of Hank tore poor Lindsey to pieces. The defense had clearly paid him a lot of money and cleaned him up, even buying him a suit to cover his tattoos and piercings, cutting his hair, and coaching him. He said he left Lindsey because she was "Irresponsible and very slutty." He pulled up some nude, very descriptive pictures of Lindsey, saying she wanted to be a *Penthouse* or *Hustler* model. Still, they wouldn't take her because she was *Too sleazy.* He was clearly trailer trash, but the defense coached him well. He was a compelling liar and really out to get Lindsey.

During cross-examination, I couldn't contain myself—the 3PT was out the door. I seemed to imagine that Buddha was telling me this guy was evil with no redeeming qualities. Suddenly, I became a *Wrathful Buddha.* I didn't know what *Wrathful Buddha* was, but I intuitively knew it was the right thing to do.

Hank's motives were only to continue to torture Lindsey while getting paid for it. His two favorite ways of causing pain and making a quick buck were lying for a living.

Normally, I would be overcome by emotion and anger in the face of injustice, but I needed to be vigilant... I tore him a new one during the cross-examination. Ordinarily, my rage would take control as I hated this guy for what he did to Lindsey and their son. Typically, I would lose rapport with the jury during one of these rage-filled sessions. Hank sold his soul (to the extent that he had one) to the devil for a few bucks. I went straight for the jugular, this time with the *wrathful energy* of Buddha. It gave those viewing the outward appearance of incredible strength without the normal accompanying anger, but inwardly, I was calm and dynamic, and my examination was on point! The best I'd ever done! My inner strength was on fire. I was Gerry Spence synergized with Hulk Hogan, smoothed by the serenity of a 350-pound gorilla mothering her babies.

While I was doing great as a *Wrathful Buddha* and thought I had things under control, the *Buddha Field* courtroom turned on a dime and changed into a *Hell Realm.* The pictures were excluded from the jury viewing them, but the damage was done.

Lindsey started balling and ran out of the courtroom. Suddenly, everything was chaotic. I was blindsided and devastated. Lindsey swore at me, screaming that I wasn't protecting her. My *Buddha Suit* was on the floor in shreds. Trying to maintain my composure, I examined Hank and asked him if he paid child support, saw his kids, had a criminal record, and had a drinking problem. I asked him if he was paid to be here. He answered, "Just the usual witness fee under the law." I didn't have time to prepare for any further information on this witness for cross-examination.

Most of my questions were met with cocky, evasive responses. The defense objected to everything, but His Honor overruled most of them and grew increasingly annoyed. Hank's vitriol and motive were so strong, I feared his testimony might be compelling to the jury. He was so clearly coached and paid, but I couldn't prove anything.

I asked him again if he was paid to be on the stand. He answered again that he had been paid just the usual witness fee under the law.

"How much was that?" I asked.

"Forty dollars and expenses."

"And how much was that?"

He scoffed, "I don't know; we'll figure it out later."

The jury looked angry, but at whom? Their energy was palpable, and with my new *Buddha Senses*, it felt like they were radiating fire and hurling fiery barbs around the room. I wasn't sure; part of me felt they sided with the defense and were disgusted with Lindsey. The defense attorney smiled smugly at me after the jury had cleared and made threats to go after Lindsey for costs and both of us for malicious prosecution.

When I hadn't heard from Sonia in days, my heart sank. Late that night, I got a text from her saying she didn't think we could maintain the relationship and wasn't sure if she was going to come over because she was emotional. I thought we weren't working out and that it should be over. There was also a text from Lindsey saying she was done because I didn't protect her and that she wasn't going to show up the next day. She would settle for anything or nothing at all. My world was crumbling again.

I maintained my composure and decided to re-employ 3PT. That night, I spent over an hour considering the Techniques that I was a Buddha, the world was a *Buddha Field,* and everybody was a Buddha in it. I felt better, but was still shell-shocked by the witness and Lindsey's reaction.

I slept surprisingly well out of pure exhaustion. I awoke the next day feeling sorry for myself. I called Lindsey and told her she had to show up because she had to be there to settle on the record and not risk a directed verdict or sanctions for failure to be there.

I emailed the defense lawyer that morning to see if he'd settle. He offered that she takes nothing, only a waiver of costs. Together with Jerry, we convinced Lindsey she had nothing to lose because she would obtain nothing since they had withdrawn all offers.

Caught up in this swirl of lying and ugly emotions, I felt an overwhelming love for Sonia. She was pure goodness; seeing her as the Buddha was easy. We were in an ideal fantasy land of Fiji. "What is this real?" I ask myself. I'd been hurt so badly in the past. I was cynical. I was reminded of the quote from *Desiderata:* "Neither be cynical about love, for in the face of all aridity and disenchantment; it is as perennial as the grass…"

My heart had been wounded, twisted. I was confused, but I decided to trust. I told Sonia how deeply I felt connected to her and that we needed to take the plunge and see one another. I offered to buy her a plane ticket and told her she could stay as long as she wanted. I was compassionate but not compulsive or pushy. The Buddha was guiding me only to seek love and the truth.

Going into the courtroom, I was determined to employ the 3PT. I saw everything was *Buddhaful: t*he judge, the jury, even the defense lawyer, and the defendant were all Buddhas. We went through closing instructions, and I did my closing argument. I argued hard and used The Three Priceless Techniques by viewing the entire jury as Buddha. My argument flowed, and at one point, I looked at them, and all their faces were that of Buddha smiling patiently at me. I maintained my composure, went over the evidence, and dealt with the damaging evidence by saying Mr. Wilcox visibly had an ax to grind.

The jury was composed of eight women and four men. They were mostly older and relatively conservative. I was speculating as to who would be the foreperson. There was a more senior, retired cop and a middle-aged housewife who appeared to be strong. I thought one of them would be the foreperson. A younger, millennial hipster was really paying attention to the evidence during the trial, with beady, angry eyes behind his round John Lennon glasses and cool duds. I was surprised and scared to see that he was selected as the foreperson as he seemed dead set against us.

After the closing argument, I felt a big pit in my stomach and a sense of defeat because the Jury didn't look me in the eyes during my closing statement and rebuttal. I had pretty much chalked it up as a loss and that I would lose Sonia at the same time as well.

(Rod Stewart's *Three Time Loser* got stuck in my head as the jury left the room. I like Rod Stewart, and I like that song, but it was too much: *I'm a three-time loser/Caught it up in Monterey/Shook it up in East Virginia/But now my friends say it's here to stay/I'm a three-time loser.*[10])

The jury took the case to the jury room on a Wednesday afternoon and deliberated on the special verdict for the rest of the afternoon. They deliberated all of Thursday and asked some questions about some of the jury instructions concerning liability. I was sure that both Lindsey and I were there for the jury to see us as they deliberated. I sensed dissection with the Jury.

As Tom Petty sang, "The waiting is the hardest part." The waiting for me was sitting in the courtroom or preferably outside in the hall, waiting for the jury to return. Most people roam nervously between the courtroom and the hallway, anxiously anticipating their fate. That

[10] "Three Time Loser," Rod Stewart, (Atlantic Crossing), 1975. These lines are excerpted from the song; all rights to the original composition and recording are reserved by the artists and distributors.

afternoon, at about 4:15 p.m., we were jarred by two buzzes from the clerk, signifying the jury had reached their verdict.

My heart was racing a week before Thanksgiving, with perfect November Indian Summer weather in Southern California. Judge Schneider said, "My Judicial staff has to leave at 4:30 p.m. sharp." And he ordered the Jury to return at 9:00 a.m. the next day. I was on pins and needles all afternoon, evening, and night, especially the following morning. I was encouraged that the Jury was out for a day and a half. I felt that if they had defended us, they would have to come back within an hour or two, but you never really know. I decided to take the verdict in stride, thinking it would be adverse toward Lindsey. I would just have to lick my wounds, pick up the pieces, and move on, expecting the worst and hoping for the best.

That morning, after a few delays, with the court hearing other matters and one juror arriving late, the clerk called the Jury into the Jury box. I hyperventilated, just wanting to get it over with. Judge Schneider asked the *hipster millennial*, which will probably be condensed to *hipsterllennial* one day, if the jury has reached a verdict. He responded, "We have, your Honor."

Things went incredibly calm, and my mind went blank. It was almost an out-of-body experience, and I saw everything in gold with a few dispersed rainbows. Suddenly, the Buddha arose in the courtroom, gazing upon me.

Going over the special verdict, the jury answered the first question in the affirmative, saying that there was a hostile environment and that the Defendant sexually harassed Lindsey. Then came the damages phase. They awarded $725,000 in compensatory damages, but that wasn't it. They also stated that the acts were despicable, shocking to the conscience, base, vile, obnoxious, and then punitive damages were awarded. There would be another phase of punitive damages to determine the amount to punish and deter defendants from such conduct based on the circumstances and their net worth, which was substantial.

Lindsey had tears in her eyes, and she hugged me. Jerry was elated. I felt so good; indeed, this was legal napalm: It smelled like… *Victory!* The Buddha slowly faded away from the courtroom, disappearing with a Cheshire Cat look of approval and a thumbs up! We will have to return on Monday for the second phase.

This would involve the number of punitive damages, and the defendant would have to disclose his net worth, which we knew was substantial, $10,000,000–$15,000,000. After that, we could get attorney fees under the Federal Employment and Housing Act and interest and costs as we beat our statutory offer to compromise, awarding us that in a penalty hearing.

Also, we beat a meager statutory offer to compromise that Jerry had made at the beginning of the lawsuit for $100,000. We were entitled to 10% interest from the time the offer expired because the defendants didn't accept it and all our costs, including experts.

The defendants and their team looked pissed, worried, scared, and embarrassed. As the day went by, I felt so good, elated, and walking on air. I immediately got hold of Sonia, and she apologized and said she was just overly emotional and scared, not wanting to get hurt again. I told her how beautiful every part of her being was and that I would never hurt her. I told her that the Bali yoga teaching job could wait and I'd pay for her to come over as long as she liked. I emphasized that we needed to give this a try to see if it was the real thing.

Over the weekend, the defense lawyer who previously ignored me or was too arrogant to talk with me was feverishly emailing me and texting me with egg on his face. I told him to call me. Honestly, it was so that I could subtly gloat. I was in the driver's seat. I felt so emboldened and confident when he called me, warming up to me and saying, "How are you, Dale?" like we were long-lost buddies.

(The soul music here was *Ain't Nothing Like the Real Thing* with Marvin Gaye Feat. Tammi Terrell: *So glad we go the real thing baby/ So glad we go the real thing/Oh honey/Ain't nothing like the real thing baby/No darling/Ain't nothing like the real thing.*[11])

Finally, he offered the defendant a million-dollar policy limit. I told Lindsey and Jerry to hold off. I told the Defense that the defendant himself would be liable for exemplary or punitive damages that wouldn't be covered under his policy to "punish and deter" future bad acts. I also told the lawyer that he may be liable for not protecting his client and should have had independent counsel. The defense was very conciliatory and polite. I had all the leverage in the world. I told him just to show up on Monday morning with his client's net worth as the Judge had ordered.

On late Sunday night, we settled for $1,250,000, with the defendant paying $250,000 out of his own pocket. We were all ecstatic. Lindsey asked what all this meant to her. I told her about $700,000, give or take. She was speechless! We appeared the following morning and told the court we had a chance to poll and talk to the jury. They voted 10-2 in our favor, were complimentary of me, and saw right through the defense and their gamesmanship.

The Judge put the settlement on the record. He glanced at me, all-knowingly. Buddha was on our side. He was very calm and seemed to think this was the correct result. He complimented both lawyers, but looked at me when he was talking. I was able to talk to some of the jurors. They were empathetic to Lindsey and said they didn't like or believe the defendants. They said I presented the case well; some even asked me for my business card. I invited Jerry and the client to brunch.

[11] "Ain't Nothing Like the Real Thing," Marvin Gaye and Tammi Terrell, (You're All I Need), 1968. These lines are excerpted from the song; all rights to the original composition and recording are reserved by the artists and distributors.

To top it all off, Sonia had booked her flight for the coming Wednesday. She'd be crossing the International Dateline and arriving Wednesday afternoon. It was indeed one of the best days of my life! It was *Buddhaful!*

Thanksgiving was coming, and there was much to be thankful for. More than ever.

Like a dream come true, Sonia arrived, and it took her a bit to clear customs. For both of us, it was pure bliss. We spent the next few weeks stuck together like magnets. She had never been to the United States, so a Golden State road trip was the go. I wanted to show her the incredible sights and natural splendors of California—the coast and all of its wonders. We drove to San Francisco, the Wine Country, Muir Woods, Mount Shasta, all the way across the border into Oregon. We camped, hiked in the Sierra, and passed through Yosemite on the way back. Time together with her was pure magic, even better than Fiji. Just as much natural beauty and stars, but no pretensions or inhibitions.

We gave each other our hearts entirely. I remember seeing pictures in Buddhist books of *Thangkas*, which are Buddhist artwork with two Buddhas in a divine union. We both felt this ecstasy as Sonia was practicing the 3PTs along with me. Visualizing each other as Buddhas in *Buddha Field* magnified the bliss many times over. It felt like our collective *Buddha Field* was the size of Los Angeles. We talked endlessly and openly, and my heart was open and pure after I embraced the three priceless techniques.

We got along so well that Sonia decided to stay as we both wanted to settle down, and she was eager to have a child. I was so ready and happy that we left Yosemite on a beautiful early summer afternoon. I looked over and saw the Buddha ever so clearly. He again gave me a warm look of pride and approval. It all began to dawn on me that my entire life—from my childhood to my adolescence to college and law school, even to Bianca and my dreams, my vacation with Todd, and all the lessons I learned in between—was all preparing me for this!

My new beginning is with my beautiful Sonia, and my new life in the Buddha Fields was quite the victory after all these trials and tribulations. The Buddha patiently watched while I reflected on my past. He gave me a moment to process all that had transpired. He said he'd keep his eyes on me and that my journey with the 3PT had just begun. While they were simple to understand, perfecting them would be a journey of time, process, and mistakes, but with commitment, it would benefit me and all sentient beings on their path to Buddhahood. And, with that, he disappeared.

Closing Statement: Life Post Verdict

About four and a half years have passed since winning Lindsey's case. There is nothing like a good verdict to boost your confidence. Also, some of the local legal rags picked it up, and I shamelessly published it in the interest of self-promotion, and it worked. My career took off. I had a string of decent verdicts and took a couple of bumps and bruises on the way to a fulfilling, wonderful, lucrative career as a boutique litigator.

I got some great settlements and rebuilt a reputation as a no-nonsense but easygoing trial lawyer badass. Not always well deserved, I often thought to myself. However, I made a lot of clients happy, and we all made money in the plaintiff's world.

More importantly, it was gratifying to really do something meaningful. I got involved in the plaintiffs' bar with some of my former enemies (now best buddies), who often chortled about what a *Supremely arrogant little dick* I used to be. I could see that now with amazing clarity through the Buddha's eyes.

Indeed, I incorporated the *Buddha's Three Priceless Techniques* into everything I did.

Throughout the sailing journey, which proved to be the most powerful agent of change (sea change) in my life, I also practiced visualization. I envisioned and committed my vision to writing. Mostly on the trip, I wrote the following goals:

1. Have a successful career that you love. Help people and make lots of money for everyone who is doing the right thing with your Buddha-given talents.
2. Live a healthy life. Meditate daily and envision your fantasy future. Be good to others and yourself. Take care of your body by doing what you love: surf, play tennis, ski, hike, work out, and eat good, pure, and wholesome foods in moderation to savor.
3. Settle down and have a family. Find the love of your life, and you will be the perfect match for one another. Have a child and live blissfully as a family.

These were simple fundamental goals that I continued to write out and refine: my goals to reflect on my ideal life where I could live by my own rules. There wasn't someone always seeking to undermine me on the other side or within the *Family Firm.*

Funny, I had faced Owens and Owens several times, which invariably confused judges and even jurors. I tried a business dispute case with pretty straightforward facts against my old foe, Greg Horowitz. It wasn't a complicated case. Anyone with any common sense could see my guy got screwed on a boring business dispute when the facts and contract clearly favored my client. Horowitz was so smug and didn't expect me to show up with the Buddha, who always had my back.

Anyway, I pulled off a $725,000 verdict from a $50,000 offer. At that point, I just wanted to prove a point, and my client "Stan"—who was well off and sophisticated—was in total agreement, and so was the jury, for that matter. It was an 11-1 verdict, with one idiot asleep at the wheel. Even the jury secretly joked to me about juror number 12, who seemed to live in a parallel universe.

Yes, if you get nine to twelve people who don't care or understand, you're out of luck. Lady Luck was on my side. Horowitz saw the jurors ask for my card while ignoring him, and he ate a slice of humble pie.

I tried hard to reverse my formerly egocentric, base personality from controlling the fundamental good I had deeply in my heart.

Walking out of the courtroom, Greg hustled up to me, extending his hand. I hesitated, smiled, and then disarmed him with a brotherly hug. I had learned to swallow the tough pill of forgiveness. We both suggested grabbing a coffee at the hot new Surf Coffee Store right in front of us. Greg opened up to me, and we became fast friends. I understood the immense family pressure and how his path was much more difficult than mine, and he was only slightly more of a jerk. He referred me to cases, and we kept on friendly terms. I had also learned about the art of compassion on my ever-expanding journey with *the 3PTs.*

Oh, I almost forgot… The most blissful part. Sonia and I are happily in a life partnership. We always wanted to have a child. However, considering our ages and overpopulation, we decided to adopt. Through a rigorous process and several months, we were blessed to adopt a one-and-a-half-year-old baby girl from South Korea named Taylor. She is the light of our life, and we have bonded as a tight family unit. She is adorable as she is walking and beginning to talk. Her smile lights up my life, and Sonia is very maternal, so she is very blessed to have a little companion, too. We are in love and seem aligned on all fronts: spirituality and sports. She picked up tennis and got quite good, so we now play against each other and also doubles. We eat wholesome, pure food, practice yoga daily, and lead a happy and healthy lifestyle.

She and I have a good life, and I get to surf whenever I want without accounting to anyone or billable hours, for that matter. Travels have taken me to some magical surf destinations. The family often goes with me, or I go with friends, and a few times, I have gone alone on reflective self-surf trips where I always vibe with the people.

In short, we are living happily ever after. Sure, there are issues here and there, and sometimes it seems the Buddha in me forgets his principles, but all in all, life has been and continues to be beautiful.

Peace.

About the Authors

Daniel of www.DanielPOHara.com started his business career as a licensed stockbroker and Commodity Trader at the age of 19, shortly before the crash of ‘87.

Experiencing the stress of high finance during turbulent times and at an early age, he found that his martial arts training didn’t give him the tools to handle the burdens of such heavy stress.

He later studied under a real-life Yoda, who taught him high levels of meditation, energy healing, and wisdom from many spiritual traditions.

Daniel is the author of five other books *Buddha Fields, Buddha Fields for Addictions, Christ’s Castle, Krishna’s Kingdom,* and *Tantric Golf. CHRISTIFICATION, Finding the Kingdom of God Within* is in process.

Daniel has led the largest meditation group in Orange County, CA, since ‘99 and is now on Zoom weekly on Thursday nights. For more information, check out www.OCMeditationGroup.com.

This book aims to move you along the path and start employing high-level meditation practices, such as the *Buddha Fields Blessing Meditation and his ESSENTIAL BUDDHIST Practices, BUDDHAFICATION, CHRISTIFICATION, and AVATARFICATION Master Classes*. Please explore his meditation, seminars, and master classes at www.DanielPOHara.com.

David Olan is a seasoned trial attorney and passionate surfer, well-known in Malibu surf circles and publications. After a successful legal career, he stepped back to embrace his love for surfing, favoring "more tubes, less cubicles." He still runs the firm and loves the law, but isn't trying cases regularly like he did previously.

Inspired by his father, a pioneering personal injury lawyer, Olan knew he wanted to be an attorney from a young age. He earned a Political Science degree from UCLA in 1985 and a Juris Doctor from the University of San Diego School of Law in 1989, where he achieved honors in the Moot Court and the International Law Society. He studied at the University of Salzburg in Austria for his junior year. He also studied in Mexico City and again in Salzburg for the summers after his 1st and 2nd year in Law School. He speaks both German and Spanish.

Olan has received numerous accolades, including Best Lawyers in America (2011–2019), Southern California Super Lawyer (2007–2019), and Top 100 Super Lawyers in Southern California for many years. He has been rated AV1 (the highest honor for skills and ethics) from Martindale-Hubbell and has been a member of the prestigious American Board of Trial Advocates for over 20 years. He's served on various legal boards and associations and is particularly proud of founding the now-international yet defunct US Association of Surfing Lawyers. He was the president of the Santa Monica Bar Association established in 1928 from 2013 to 2014.

Now, David is co-owner of SeaNSoul (www.SeaNSoul.com), a fabulous, popular Surf, Coffee, and Clothing Store located in Zuma Plaza across from the beach in Malibu.

Contact authors at:

david@olanlaw.com

www.olanlaw.com

Praise Continued

"Dave Olan started the Association of Surfing Lawyers over twenty years ago. It has now become international. I met Dave when he started ASL. When I prepared my presentation as a guest speaker for the nascent surfing lawyers in 2002, it was an inspiration and catalyst for my book *The 10 Commandments of Surfing*.

Shaun Tomson was flying at the Bay of Plenty circa 1978.
Photo: Jeff Divine.

Surfing has gone hand-in-hand with spiritual growth and enlightenment. The practice of law does not focus on those beautiful sentiments. Dave's book, *The Enlightened Lawyer,* has blended his love for surfing and passion for the law.

The Enlightened Lawyer: Three Priceless Techniques to Transform Your Life is a fascinating, exciting story of adventure—a good read for anyone who is a lawyer, surfer, spiritualist, or someone who needs a path to a more meaningful, satisfying life."

—Shaun Tomson, World Champion Surfer,
Inspirational Speaker, Author of *Surfer's Code*,
Owner of Instinct Surf Company

"In *The Enlightened Lawyer*, seasoned attorney and Malibu surfer Dale Owen falls victim to a bloodcurdling scam, nearly disgraces his family's firm, and plummets through hell, where he ultimately learns that "the Buddha's always got your back." This totally unique 'West-looks-East' story is told with tenderness, humor, and a true surfer's eye for peril and grace under pressure—awesome reading for anyone reaching for higher ground."

—Daniel Weizmann,
Author of *The Last Songbird*
& *Cinnamon Girl*

"*The Enlightened Lawyer: Three Priceless Techniques to Transform Your Life* by Dave Olan skillfully merges legal drama with a journey of spiritual awakening and oceanic adventure. The story follows Dale Owen, a successful attorney whose life unravels due to both professional challenges and personal crises. Bianca, a former client, lures Dale in through her intoxicating attraction, only to blindside him, causing his life to go into a tailspin. The narrative vividly depicts Dale's decline, making his subsequent spiritual rebirth even more impactful.

Dale's transformation begins when he encounters a mystical Buddha figure who imparts the Three Priceless Techniques. These teachings guide Dale to embrace his own Buddha nature, perceive the world as a sacred space, and view others as fellow spiritual beings. The book is not only a story of redemption but also a practical guide to integrating spiritual wisdom into everyday life, particularly for those navigating the stresses of a demanding career.

Olan's writing is engaging and insightful, making complex spiritual concepts accessible and relatable. The novel also emphasizes the healing power of nature, particularly the sea, which aligns with the spiritual lessons Dale learns. *The Enlightened Lawyer* is a powerful exploration of the resilience of the human spirit and the potential for growth and enlightenment, making it an essential read for anyone seeking to balance professional success with personal and spiritual growth."

—Mitch Stone, Celebrity Hairdresser,
Photographer, and Author

"*The Enlightened Lawyer: Three Priceless Techniques to Transform Your Life* is a remarkable and honest story of one man's journey from success and privilege to failure and loss and back again. It is the story of how his road to redemption was inspired by the convergence of two seemingly unrelated phenomena: the mystical, deeply transformative power of surfing and the unexpected appearance of the Buddha, who presents him with a jewel of immeasurable wisdom with which to change his life, his mind, and his destiny—the *Three Priceless Techniques*.

In his crafting of this story's protagonist, author David Olan presents us with the perfect archetype embodying our culture's contemporary vision of the successful alpha male—a man fixated on amassing wealth, obsessed with winning at any cost, and oblivious to the value of human relationships as anything other than transactional exchanges. We meet Dale Owen, a man mired in the egocentric world of contentious litigation, deriving both his livelihood and his self-worth through the deployment of aggression, hostility, and occasionally even dishonesty in his quest to prevail over an opponent. He also holds a regressive view of women, reducing them to mere *accouterments* whose purpose is to soothe, satisfy, and enhance the male ego. As the Universe often does, this toxic belief manifests itself in the form of an actual *femme fatale* of incredible beauty who walks into Dale's office one day and changes the trajectory of his entire life, bestowing euphoria, sexual fulfillment and illusions of grandeur but leaves devastation, financial ruin, and deep emotional damage in her wake.

And it's there, in the charnel grounds of psychological, physical, and emotional Hell that our hero encounters *the Buddha* of infinite compassion, who benevolently and without judgment teaches Dale how to transform his life by transforming himself and his relationship with the world around him. Utilizing the *Three Priceless Techniques* from author Daniel O'Hara's *Buddha Fields for Attorneys* series, the story follows Dale's journey as he confronts his true nature and discovers—as Buddhism teaches—the inherent goodness within himself and the *Buddha nature* inherent in all people. As he applies the techniques and rediscovers the magical and healing power of *he'e nalu* (surfing), he heals his relationships with family and with women in deep and meaningful ways. With humor and raw honesty, *The Enlightened Lawyer* is a moving and delightful story that reminds us that no matter where we think we are in the world—whether on top of it or sinking beneath the waves—we are all Buddhas, worthy of compassion and forgiveness, and capable of profound goodness and compassion toward others."

—Lauryn Boston, Attorney/Mediator, Long-Time Maui Resident, and Buddhist, Co-creator of John from Cincinnati and Chance, Writer on HBO's Deadwood and FX's Sons of Anarchy

"In *The Enlightened Lawyer*, David Olan takes you through the very real and challenging life of a lawyer whose life turns upside down overnight. While facing numerous challenges and faced with the prospect of losing everything he has ever worked for, Dale Owen turns to waves and is washed with the messages of Buddha. Dale's transformation from a heartless, billing-machine, mundane lawyer to an enlightened advocate is so beautiful, heartwarming, and touching. The Three Priceless Techniques adopted by David truly serve as a model for not just us lawyers but should be practiced by everyone in order to achieve a more meaningful and fulfilling life. I highly recommend *The Enlightened Lawyer* to everyone."

—Tawny Mazarei, California Attorney,
Advocate for Justice and Fair Business Practice

"*The Enlightened Lawyer: Three Priceless Techniques to Transform Your Life* by Dave Olan is a captivating blend of legal drama, spiritual awakening, and oceanic adventure. The book offers a unique exploration of the tumultuous life of Dale Owen, a high-powered attorney whose journey from the pinnacle of legal success to the depths of despair and back again is both compelling and instructive. It effectively combines the intensity of legal drama with a profound spiritual journey and the healing power of nature.

Dale Owen's story begins in the fast-paced, high-stress world of a family-run law firm. Despite his professional success, Dale's personal life is a mess. Entangled in the vices symbolized by the Seven Deadly Sins, Dale's downfall is precipitated by his ill-fated romance with Bianca, a femme fatale who lures him into a catastrophic scam.

Olan's depiction of Dale's downward spiral is raw and realistic, making his subsequent spiritual rebirth all the more poignant. The turning point in Dale's journey comes with the intervention of a mystical Buddha figure, who imparts the Three Priceless Techniques. These techniques serve as the foundation for Dale's transformation, urging him to recognize his own Buddha nature, perceive the world as a Buddha Field, and see others as Buddhas on their path.

The Enlightened Lawyer is a multifaceted narrative that offers more than just a story of personal redemption. It is a guide to integrating spiritual wisdom into everyday life, especially for those caught in the relentless grind of professional obligations. Olan's writing is both engaging and instructive, making complex spiritual concepts accessible and relatable. *The Enlightened Lawyer* is a thought-provoking and inspiring read. The novel beautifully interweaves these spiritual teachings with the therapeutic power of nature, particularly the sea. Olan eloquently captures the serenity and healing potential of the ocean, aligning it with the ancient wisdom of the Three Priceless Techniques.

Dale Owen's transformation is a testament to the resilience of the human spirit and the potential for redemption and enlightenment in even the most challenging circumstances. This book is a must-read for anyone seeking insight into balancing professional success with personal fulfillment and spiritual growth."

—James Carr,
International Trial Lawyer

"Dave Olan is an accomplished waterman, an excellent attorney, and a good friend, always willing to go above and beyond in pursuit of justice for those lucky enough to find their way into his orbit. In *The Enlightened Lawyer,* he is after big game, tackling some of life's most fundamental questions, and finally, taking on one of life's greatest challenges: How, in Nietzsche's formulation, to become who you are. *The Enlightened Lawyer* is recommended reading for anyone seeking balance amid life's ever-shifting waves."

—Kem Nunn, Creator of "surf noir," Author of
Tapping the Source*, *Tijuana Straits*, *John from Cincinnati,
Co-creator of John from Cincinnati and Chance,
Writer on HBO's Deadwood and FX's Sons of Anarchy

"As a "recovering lawyer" who practiced for over twenty-five years, but during that time was also an artist, spiritualist, and cancer survivor, and who now is a bookstore owner, life coach, and founder of a crystal and geode gallery, I wholeheartedly agree with David's approach to life—balance, in all that we do, is key to health, happiness, and fulfillment.

—Jeffrey Segal, Recovering Lawyer,
Owner of Mystic Journey in Santa Monica, California

"Dave Olan is a serious surfer and lawyer—but not necessarily in that order, depending on the situation at hand. He's pursued both with passion and commitment, and his life and work reflect a thoughtful sense of accomplishment, purpose, and joy. Surfing is all about maintaining perfect balance, and Dave has sought the same sense of ideal centeredness by deftly integrating his water time with the demands of a competitive profession and successful business. He is an original surfing lawyer and has packed this entertaining tale with many insights on a subject well worth examining every day of our too-busy modern lives."

—John DeCure, State Bar Prosecutor, Administrative
Law Judge, Author of *Reef Dance* and *Bluebird Rising*

"I know, Dave! I've surfed with Dave and he was cool out in the lineup! And Dave won me a lot of money in a lawsuit when I lost everything in the Woolsey fire in Malibu! I like Dave, he's a lawyer who surfs!"

—John Philbin, aka Turtle from *North Shore*,
aka Nathanial from *Point Break*

John Philbin training Kate Bosworth how to walk the walk and talk the talk and paddle like a surfer for the 2002 movie Blue Crush. Photo courtesy: John Philbin.

"The salient point made in the narrative of *The Enlightened Lawyer* is recalled in the Judaic tradition of Psalms: "Those that know the Lord are the ones that go down to the ocean and journey in its depths."

According to "Halacha," or Talmudic dictum, there are three sources of curative and ritual means of purification for one who has become spiritually impure: a natural, active, fresh-water spring whose volume is at least forty gallons; a "mikva" or body of water collected by raindrops whose volume is at least forty gallons; and immersion of the entire body into the ocean.

My inquiry into this last source of spiritual purification has lasted my entire surfing career since that first fateful day of my immersion into the fabled waves of Malibu Beach in 1962.

The ignominious path of attorney Dale, the protagonist of this worthy and timeless tale, and his downward drift into the web of debauchery suffered by so many in our ever-imploding society, can be viewed by the soul surfer as a form of death, far away from the uplifting and spiritually emancipating life of the ocean and its treasured waves. Surfing is scoffed at by most who are driven by the quest for money and power, usually in terms of being a "waste of time." Yet, the redemptive and spiritually uplifting power and majesty of the waves is the true source of life for many, the cure to what ails modern man and the purifying agent that arights the soul on its earthly journey.

Rabbi Nachum Shifren going with the flow at Malibu.
Photo: Yahweh.

The Enlightened Lawyer is nothing less than an ode to the path of righteousness and holistic living as exemplified by the essence of the act of surfing and its associated lifestyle. For those who have traversed a world of falsity and dubious ways of existence, this book is nothing less than a rescue manual of how-to steps to personal redemption and a holistic lifestyle.

Kudos to author and Attorney David Olan for his curative work which should be required reading for every lawyer!"

—Shaloha, Rabbi Nachum Shifren,
Author of *Surfing Rabbi & Surfers Who Don't Surf*

"In Dora v. Frontline Video, Inc., 15 Cal. App. 4th 536, 546 (Cal. Ct. App. 1993), the California Appeals Court stated: *Having said that, we find that surfing is of more than passing interest to some. It has created a lifestyle that influences speech, behavior, dress, and entertainment, among other things. A phenomenon of such scope has an economic impact because it affects purchases, travel, and the housing market. Surfing has also had a significant influence on the popular culture, and in that way touches many people.*

Dave Olan is the epitome of what the State of California Courts have acknowledged and what we all, as surfers, intuitively know. This so-called stoner pastime has become bigger and of broader scope than anyone would have ever imagined. And to Dave's credit, he's successfully ridden the world's best waves and along the way, confronted risk, danger, bad odds, unruly crowds, etc., with grace and balance. Oh… and he's done the same thing in courtrooms across the West for decades. As Enlightened Lawyer demonstrates, surfers can do law, and lawyers can surf."

—Mark Massara, Surfer and Pioneer
Environmental Warrior/Lawyer

"Our profession is only part of our personality and cannot define our true nature and character. Therefore, The Enlightened Lawyer is a sincere shared life experience for all the people who do not allow to be swallowed by the nature of their profession... any profession!"

—Aleksandar Damchevski, Republic of Macedonia, Attorney at Law with Management Experience (by Profession), Personal Trainer and Musician Solo Performer in Las Vegas (by Passion)

"Dave walks his talk. He also does so with a perfect Austrian dialect from his time as a child going to University of Salzburg in our beautiful mother land.

The Enlightened Lawyer captures the essence and vibe of our protagonist, Dale's, legal career highlighting his anecdotal adventurous experiences.

It is a profound allegorical tale of a journey many of us have traveled from despair to Enlightenment. Dale employs the 3 priceless techniques on his path towards his spiritual awakening. It is well written, clever, and moving. A real page Turner. I highly recommend reading it."

—Sigmar Berg, Author of One Journey,
Athlete from Austria, Founder of Love Tuner
(www.lovetuner.com)

"I loved the way the book flowed and how I could relate to the stories and the movie quotes from some of my favorites. The book seemed believable and definitely relatable to me and the environment I grew up in. I recommend this book to anyone looking for some insight and inspiration."

—Jeff De Prez, CEO/Founder
DPS Property Services

"Dale Owen is a captivating fictional character, inspired by the remarkable life of the distinguished and extraordinary attorney, David Olan, who is also an accomplished surfer. This book is an essential addition for legal professionals aspiring to lead a fulfilling and self-actualized lifestyle while effectively navigating the complexities of their clients' legal matters. Providing a blueprint for excellence both in the courtroom and in life, Dale Owen's story serves as an inspiring guide for those committed to achieving success and balance in their legal careers."

—Jose Angel Manaiza Jr., Mathematician and Tutor to The Stars voted as The Best of Los Angeles Awards